Keto Diet

Book with 30-Day Meal Plan

Delicious Recipes with Low Carb to Lose Weight, Quick & Easy Low-Carb Homemade Cooking, incl. Sides, Snacks, Desserts & More

Charles S. Campos

CONTENTS

Chapter 4: Fish And Seafood Recipes 35

Chapter 7: Desserts And Drinks Recipes 72

30 Day Meal Plan.. 84

Appendix : Recipes Index 86

INTRODUCTION

Hello everyone! Thanks for buying this cookbook. My name is Charles S. Campos, I am a dietitian specializing in healthy eating and effective weight loss. After getting my dietitian license, I started writing healthy recipes for people. Making a 30-Day healthy eating plan for my mom, because she was upset due to obesity for many years. She is gradually recovered and weight loss with my keto recipes. This keto diet cookbook is good enough for everyone! <Keto Diet Book with 30-Day Meal Plan> is my first cookbook. Please follow me to learn how to make healthy and delicious food with keto diet.

This Keto Diet Book begins with a brief introduction of keto diet, which can help you to make easy and delicious food. There is a great deal of keto recipes in the cookbook, which are applicable to your every meal. Each recipe also has detailed directions, a clear list of ingredients, cooking temperature and time, so you don't have to worry about anything and just follow step by step.

Chapter 1 : Keto Diet

What Is Keto Diet?

This Keo Diet Cookbook is featuring a low-carbohydrate, high-quality fat diet. 1500+ easy-to-follow, well-tested keto recipes and dishes to suit your tastes, from breakfast to dinner to dessert, with useful information such as nutritional value, preparation time and cooking instructions designed to delight taste buds and promote health.

A detailed 30-Day Meal Plan to get you started, with comprehensive shopping and food lists, and tips for creating your own menus. Whether you want to start the day with a hearty breakfast or wind down with a delectable dinner, you'll find flavorful and nourishing recipes like Zucchini And Cheese Gratin, Cranberry Sauce Meatballs. Step-by-Step Instructions. A wide variety of deliciously healthy keto diet recipes, with most needing minimal cook and prep time!

What Does A Keto Diet Involve?

1. Per capita daily salt intake ≤ 0.17 oz

2. The recommended intake of edible oil per adult is 0.88~1.06oz

3. The per capita intake of added sugar ≤ 0.88 oz

4. Daily intake of vegetables and fruits ≥ 17.64 oz

5. Daily intake of food ≥ 12 types

Adults maintain a healthy weight, 18.5 ≤ BMI < 24

Why You Need A Keto Diet?

A keto diet includes a combination of fruits and vegetables, whole grains and starches, high-quality fats and lean proteins, so picky eaters should change it quickly! A healthy diet should not eat too salty and sweet. Top 10 benefits of a healthy keto diet.

1. Weight loss, weight loss can help reduce the risk of chronic diseases. If a person is overweight or obese, they are at higher risk of developing several diseases.

2. Reduced risk of cancer, an unhealthy diet can lead to obesity, which may increase a person's risk of cancer. Being massed within a healthy range can reduce this risk.

3. Diabetes management, eating a healthy keto diet can help diabetics to lose weight (if needed), manage blood sugar levels, keep blood pressure and cholesterol within target range, prevent or delay diabetes complications.

4. Heart health and stroke prevention, it is evidenced that vitamin E can prevent blood clots, which can reduce the likelihood of a heart attack. The following foods contain high levels of vitamin E: almonds, peanuts, hazelnuts, sunflower seeds, green vegetables.

5. Strong bones and teeth, it must have enough calcium and magnesium. Maintaining bone health is essential to prevent osteoporosis and osteoarthritis.

6. Better mood, it is evidenced that a strong relationship between diet and mood. A healthy keto diet can improve overall mood.

You can start once you understand the benefits and science of keto diet, these recipes will provide you with what you need to succeed with the keto diet — easy cooking, weight loss, and enjoy delicious food!

Measurement Conversions

BASIC KITCHEN CONVERSIONS & EQUIVALENTS

DRY MEASUREMENTS CONVERSION CHART

3 TEASPOONS = 1 TABLESPOON = 1/16 CUP

6 TEASPOONS = 2 TABLESPOONS = 1/8 CUP

12 TEASPOONS = 4 TABLESPOONS = 1/4 CUP

24 TEASPOONS = 8 TABLESPOONS = 1/2 CUP

36 TEASPOONS = 12 TABLESPOONS = 3/4 CUP

48 TEASPOONS = 16 TABLESPOONS = 1 CUP

METRIC TO US COOKING CONVERSIONS

OVEN TEMPERATURES

120 °C = 250 °F

160 °C = 320 °F

180° C = 350 °F

205 °C = 400 °F

220 °C = 425 °F

LIQUID MEASUREMENTS CONVERSION CHART

8 FLUID OUNCES = 1 CUP = 1/2 PINT = 1/4 QUART

16 FLUID OUNCES = 2 CUPS = 1 PINT = 1/2 QUART

32 FLUID OUNCES = 4 CUPS = 2 PINTS = 1 QUART

 = 1/4 GALLON

128 FLUID OUNCES = 16 CUPS = 8 PINTS = 4 QUARTS = 1 GALLON

BAKING IN GRAMS

1 CUP FLOUR = 140 GRAMS

1 CUP SUGAR = 150 GRAMS

1 CUP POWDERED SUGAR = 160 GRAMS

1 CUP HEAVY CREAM = 235 GRAMS

VOLUME

1 MILLILITER = 1/5 TEASPOON

5 ML = 1 TEASPOON

15 ML = 1 TABLESPOON

240 ML = 1 CUP OR 8 FLUID OUNCES

1 LITER = 34 FL. OUNCES

WEIGHT

1 GRAM = .035 OUNCES

100 GRAMS = 3.5 OUNCES

500 GRAMS = 1.1 POUNDS

1 KILOGRAM = 35 OUNCES

US TO METRIC COOKING CONVERSIONS

1/5 TSP = 1 ML

1 TSP = 5 ML

1 TBSP = 15 ML

1 FL OUNCE = 30 ML

1 CUP = 237 ML

1 PINT (2 CUPS) = 473 ML

1 QUART (4 CUPS) = .95 LITER

1 GALLON (16 CUPS) = 3.8 LITERS

1 OZ = 28 GRAMS

1 POUND = 454 GRAMS

BUTTER

1 CUP BUTTER = 2 STICKS = 8 OUNCES = 230 GRAMS = 8 TABLESPOONS

WHAT DOES 1 CUP EQUAL

1 CUP = 8 FLUID OUNCES

1 CUP = 16 TABLESPOONS

1 CUP = 48 TEASPOONS

1 CUP = 1/2 PINT

1 CUP = 1/4 QUART

1 CUP = 1/16 GALLON

1 CUP = 240 ML

BAKING PAN CONVERSIONS

1 CUP ALL-PURPOSE FLOUR = 4.5 OZ

1 CUP ROLLED OATS = 3 OZ 1 LARGE EGG = 1.7 OZ

1 CUP BUTTER = 8 OZ 1 CUP MILK = 8 OZ

1 CUP HEAVY CREAM = 8.4 OZ

1 CUP GRANULATED SUGAR = 7.1 OZ

1 CUP PACKED BROWN SUGAR = 7.75 OZ

1 CUP VEGETABLE OIL = 7.7 OZ

1 CUP UNSIFTED POWDERED SUGAR = 4.4 OZ

BAKING PAN CONVERSIONS

9-INCH ROUND CAKE PAN = 12 CUPS

10-INCH TUBE PAN =16 CUPS

11-INCH BUNDT PAN = 12 CUPS

9-INCH SPRINGFORM PAN = 10 CUPS

9 X 5 INCH LOAF PAN = 8 CUPS

9-INCH SQUARE PAN = 8 CUPS

Chapter 2: Appetizers, Snacks & Side Dishes Recipes

Crunchy Pork Rind And Zucchini Sticks

Servings: 4 | Cooking Time: 20 Minutes

Ingredients:
- Cooking spray
- ¼ cup pork rind crumbs
- 1 tsp sweet paprika
- ¼ cup shredded Parmesan cheese
- Salt and chili pepper to taste
- 3 fresh eggs
- 2 zucchinis, cut into strips
- Aioli:
- ½ cup mayonnaise
- 1 garlic clove, minced
- Juice and zest from ½ lemon

Directions:
1. Preheat oven to 425ºF and line a baking sheet with foil. Grease with cooking spray and set aside. Mix the pork rinds, paprika, parmesan cheese, salt, and chili pepper in a bowl. Beat the eggs in another bowl. Coat zucchini strips in egg, then in parmesan mixture, and arrange on the baking sheet. Grease lightly with cooking spray and bake for 15 minutes to be crispy.
2. To make the aioli, combine in a bowl mayonnaise, lemon juice, and garlic, and gently stir until everything is well incorporated. Add the lemon zest, adjust the seasoning and stir again. Cover and place in the refrigerator until ready to serve. Serve the zucchini strips with garlic aioli for dipping.

Nutrition Info:
- Per Servings 2g Carbs, 6g Protein, 14g Fat, 180 Calories

Bacon Mashed Cauliflower

Servings: 6 | Cooking Time: 40 Minutes

Ingredients:
- 6 slices bacon
- 3 heads cauliflower, leaves removed
- 2 cups water
- 2 tbsp melted butter
- ½ cup buttermilk
- Salt and black pepper to taste
- ¼ cup grated yellow cheddar cheese
- 2 tbsp chopped chives

Directions:
1. Preheat oven to 350ºF. Fry bacon in a heated skillet over medium heat for 5 minutes until crispy. Remove to a paper towel-lined plate, allow to cool, and crumble. Set aside and keep bacon fat.
2. Boil cauli heads in water in a pot over high heat for 7 minutes, until tender. Drain and put in a bowl.
3. Include butter, buttermilk, salt, black pepper, and puree using a hand blender until smooth and creamy. Lightly grease a casserole dish with the bacon fat and spread the mash in it.
4. Sprinkle with cheddar cheese and place under the broiler for 4 minutes on high until the cheese melts. Remove and top with bacon and chopped chives. Serve with pan-seared scallops.

Nutrition Info:
- Per Servings 6g Carbs, 14g Protein, 25g Fat, 312 Calories

Zucchini And Cheese Gratin

Servings: 8 | Cooking Time: 15 Minutes

Ingredients:
- 5 tablespoons butter
- 1 onion, sliced
- ½ cup heavy cream
- 4 cups raw zucchini, sliced
- 1 ½ cups shredded pepper Jack cheese
- Salt and pepper to taste

Directions:
1. Place all ingredients in a mixing bowl and give a good stir to incorporate everything.
2. Pour the mixture in a heat-proof baking dish.
3. Place in a 350F preheated oven and bake for 15 minutes.
4. Serve and enjoy.

Nutrition Info:
- Per Servings 5.0g Carbs, 8.0g Protein, 20.0g Fat, 280 Calories

Cranberry Sauce Meatballs

Servings: 2 | Cooking Time: 25 Mins

Ingredients:
- 1 pound lean ground beef
- 1 egg
- 2 tablespoons water
- 1/2 cup cauliflower rice
- 3 tablespoons minced onion
- 1 can jellied cranberry sauce, keto-friendly
- 3/4 cup chili sauce

Directions:
1. Preheat oven to 350 degrees F.
2. Mix the ground beef, egg, water, cauliflower rice and minced onions together until well combined. Form into small meatballs and place on a rack over a foil-lined baking sheet.
3. Bake the meatballs for 20 to 25 minutes, turning halfway through.
4. Combine sauce ingredients in a large saucepan over low heat, toss with meatballs and allow to simmer on low for 1 hour.
5. Serve and garnish with parsley if desired.

Nutrition Info:
- Per Servings 8.6g Carbs, 9.8g Protein, 10.2g Fat, 193 Calories

Spicy Devilled Eggs With Herbs

Servings: 4 | Cooking Time: 30 Minutes

Ingredients:
- 12 large eggs
- 1 ½ cups water
- 6 tbsp mayonnaise
- Salt and chili pepper to taste
- 1 tsp mixed dried herbs
- ½ tsp sugar-free Worcestershire sauce
- ¼ tsp Dijon mustard
- A pinch of sweet paprika
- Chopped parsley to garnish
- Ice water Bath

Directions:
1. Pour the water into a saucepan, add the eggs, and bring to boil on high heat for 10 minutes. Cut the eggs in half length-ways and remove the yolks into a medium bowl. Use a fork to crush the yolks.
2. Add the mayonnaise, salt, chili pepper, dried herbs, Worcestershire sauce, mustard, and paprika. Mix together until a smooth paste has formed. Then, spoon the mixture into the piping bag and fill the egg white holes with it. Garnish with the chopped parsley and serve immediately.

Nutrition Info:
- Per Servings 0.4g Carbs, 6.7g Protein, 9.3g Fat, 112 Calories

Tuna Topped Pickles

Servings: 5 | Cooking Time: 0 Minutes

Ingredients:
- 1 tbsp fresh dill, and more for garnish
- ¼ cup full-fat mayonnaise
- 1 can light flaked tuna, drained
- 5 dill pickles
- ¼ tsp pepper

Directions:
1. Slice pickles in half, lengthwise. With a spoon, deseed the pickles and discard seeds.
2. In a small bowl, mix well the mayo, dill, and tuna using a fork.
3. Evenly divide them into 10 and spread over deseeded pickles.
4. Garnish with more dill on top and sprinkle black pepper.
5. Evenly divide into suggested servings and enjoy.

Nutrition Info:
- Per Servings 4g Carbs, 11g Protein, 14g Fat, 180 Calories

Baked Cheese & Spinach Balls

Servings: 8 | Cooking Time: 30 Minutes

Ingredients:
- ⅓ cup crumbled ricotta cheese
- ¼ tsp nutmeg
- ¼ tsp pepper
- 3 tbsp heavy cream
- 1 tsp garlic powder
- 1 tbsp onion powder
- 2 tbsp butter, melted
- ⅓ cup Parmesan cheese
- 2 eggs
- 1 cup spinach
- 1 cup almond flour

Directions:
1. Place all ingredients in a food processor. Process until smooth. Place in the freezer for about 10 minutes. Make balls out of the mixture and arrange them on a lined baking sheet. Bake at 350°F for about 10-12 minutes.

Nutrition Info:
- Per Servings 0.8g Carbs, 8g Protein, 15g Fat, 160 Calories

Baked Vegetable Side

Servings: 4 | Cooking Time: 15 Minutes

Ingredients:
- 1 large zucchini, sliced
- 1 bell pepper, sliced
- ½ cup peeled garlic cloves, sliced
- A dash of oregano
- 4 tablespoons olive oil
- Salt and pepper to taste

Directions:
1. Place all ingredients in a mixing bowl. Stir to coat everything.
2. Place in a baking sheet.
3. Bake in a 350F preheated oven for 15 minutes.
4. Serve and enjoy.

Nutrition Info:
- Per Servings 10.0g Carbs, 3.0g Protein, 23.0g Fat, 191 Calories

Zucchini Gratin With Feta Cheese

Servings: 6 | Cooking Time: 65 Minutes

Ingredients:

- Cooking spray
- 2 lb zucchinis, sliced
- 2 red bell peppers, seeded and sliced
- Salt and black pepper to taste
- 1 ½ cups crumbled feta cheese
- ⅓ cup crumbled feta cheese for topping
- 2 tbsp butter
- ¼ tsp xanthan gum
- ½ cup heavy whipping cream

Directions:

1. Preheat oven to 370ºF. Place the sliced zucchinis in a colander over the sink, sprinkle with salt and let sit for 20 minutes. Transfer to paper towels to drain the excess liquid.
2. Grease a baking dish with cooking spray and make a layer of zucchini and bell peppers in the dish overlapping one on another. Season with black pepper, and sprinkle with some feta cheese. Repeat the layering process a second time.
3. Combine the butter, xanthan gum, and whipping cream in a microwave dish for 2 minutes, stir to mix completely, and pour over the vegetables. Top with remaining feta cheese.
4. Bake the gratin for 45 minutes to be golden brown on top. Cut out slices and serve with kale salad.

Nutrition Info:

- Per Servings 4g Carbs, 14g Protein, 21g Fat, 264 Calories

Party Bacon And Pistachio Balls

Servings: 8 | Cooking Time: 45 Minutes

Ingredients:

- 8 bacon slices, cooked and chopped
- 8 ounces Liverwurst
- ¼ cup chopped pistachios
- 1 tsp Dijon mustard
- 6 ounces cream cheese

Directions:

1. Combine the liverwurst and pistachios in the bowl of your food processor. Pulse until smooth. Whisk the cream cheese and mustard in another bowl. Make 12 balls out of the liverwurst mixture.
2. Make a thin cream cheese layer over. Coat with bacon, arrange on a plate and chill for 30 minutes.

Nutrition Info:

- Per Servings 1.5g Carbs, 7g Protein, 12g Fat, 145 Calories

Old Bay Chicken Wings

Servings: 4 | Cooking Time: 30 Minutes

Ingredients:

- 3 pounds chicken wings
- ¾ cup almond flour
- 1 tablespoon old bay spices
- 1 teaspoon lemon juice, freshly squeezed
- ½ cup butter
- Salt and pepper to taste

Directions:

1. Preheat oven to 400oF.
2. In a mixing bowl, combine all ingredients except for the butter.
3. Place in an even layer in a baking sheet.
4. Bake for 30 minutes. Halfway through the cooking time, shake the fryer basket for even cooking.
5. Once cooked, drizzle with melted butter.

Nutrition Info:

- Per Servings 1.6g Carbs, 52.5g Protein, 59.2g Fat, 700 Calories

Mixed Roast Vegetables

Servings: 4 | Cooking Time: 40 Minutes

Ingredients:
- 1 large butternut squash, cut into chunks
- ¼ lb shallots, peeled
- 4 rutabagas, cut into chunks
- ¼ lb Brussels sprouts
- 1 sprig rosemary, chopped
- 1 sprig thyme, chopped
- 4 cloves garlic, peeled only
- 3 tbsp olive oil
- Salt and black pepper to taste

Directions:
1. Preheat the oven to 450ºF.
2. Pour the butternut squash, shallots, rutabagas, garlic cloves, and brussels sprouts in a bowl. Season with salt, pepper, olive oil, and toss them. Pour the mixture on a baking sheet and sprinkle with the chopped thyme and rosemary. Roast the vegetables for 15–20 minutes.
3. Once ready, remove and spoon into a serving bowl. Serve with oven roasted chicken thighs.

Nutrition Info:
- Per Servings 8g Carbs, 3g Protein, 3g Fat, 65 Calories

Spinach And Ricotta Gnocchi

Servings: 4 | Cooking Time: 13 Minutes

Ingredients:
- 3 cups chopped spinach
- 1 cup ricotta cheese
- 1 cup Parmesan cheese , grated
- ¼ tsp nutmeg powder
- 1 egg, cracked into a bowl
- Salt and black pepper
- Almond flour, on standby
- 2 ½ cups water
- 2 tbsp butter

Directions:
1. To a bowl, add the ricotta cheese, half of the parmesan cheese, egg, nutmeg powder, salt, spinach, almond flour, and pepper. Mix well. Make quenelles of the mixture using 2 tbsp and set aside.
2. Bring the water to boil over high heat on a stovetop, about 5 minutes. Place one gnocchi onto the water, if it breaks apart; add some more flour to the other gnocchi to firm it up.
3. Put the remaining gnocchi in the water to poach and rise to the top, about 2 minutes. Remove the gnocchi with a perforated spoon to a serving plate.
4. Melt the butter in a microwave and pour over the gnocchi. Sprinkle with the remaining parmesan cheese and serve with a green salad.

Nutrition Info:
- Per Servings 4.1g Carbs, 6.5g Protein, 8.3g Fat, 125 Calories

Spinach Turnip Salad With Bacon

Servings: 4 | Cooking Time: 40 Minutes

Ingredients:
- 6 turnips, cut into wedges
- 1 tsp olive oil
- 1 cup baby spinach chopped
- 3 radishes, sliced
- 3 bacon slices, sliced
- 4 tbsp sour cream
- 2 tsp mustard seeds
- 1 tsp Dijon mustard
- 1 tbsp red wine vinegar
- Salt and black pepper to taste
- 1 tbsp chopped chives

Directions:

1. Preheat the oven to 400°F. Line a baking sheet with parchment paper, toss the turnips with pepper, drizzle with the olive oil, and bake for 25 minutes, turning halfway. Let cool.

2. Spread the baby spinach in the bottom of a salad bowl and top with the radishes. Remove the turnips to the salad bowl. Fry the bacon in a skillet over medium heat until crispy, about 5 minutes.

3. Mix the sour cream, mustard seeds, Dijon mustard, vinegar, and salt with the bacon. Add a little water to deglaze the bottom of the skillet and turn off the heat.

4. Pour the bacon mixture over the vegetables, scatter the chives over it, and season with black pepper. Serve the salad with grilled pork chops.

Nutrition Info:
- Per Servings 3.1g Carbs, 9.5g Protein, 18.3g Fat, 193 Calories

Cheesy Cauliflower Fritters

Servings: 4 | Cooking Time: 35 Minutes

Ingredients:
- 1 pound grated cauliflower
- ½ cup Parmesan cheese
- 3 ounces chopped onion
- ½ tsp baking powder
- ½ cup almond flour
- 3 eggs
- ½ tsp lemon juice
- 2 tbsp olive oil
- ⅓ tsp salt

Directions:

1. Sprinkle the salt over the cauliflower in a bowl, and let it stand for 10 minutes. Add in the other ingredients. Mix with your hands to combine. Place a skillet over medium heat, and heat olive oil.

2. Shape fritters out of the cauliflower mixture. Fry in batches, for about 3 minutes per side.

Nutrition Info:
- Per Servings 3g Carbs, 4.5g Protein, 4.5g Fat, 69 Calories

Cajun Spiced Pecans

Servings: 12 | Cooking Time: 10 Minutes

Ingredients:
- 1-pound pecan halves
- ¼ cup melted butter
- 1 packet Cajun seasoning mix
- ¼ teaspoon ground cayenne pepper
- Salt and pepper to taste

Directions:
1. Preheat oven to 400oF.
2. In a small bowl, whisk well-melted butter, Cajun seasoning, cayenne, salt, and pepper.
3. Place pecan halves on a cookie sheet. Drizzle with sauce. Toss well to coat.
4. Pop in the oven and roast for 10 minutes.
5. Let it cool completely, serve, and enjoy.

Nutrition Info:
- Per Servings 5.7g Carbs, 3.5g Protein, 31.1g Fat, 297.1 Calories

Sautéed Brussels Sprouts

Servings: 4 | Cooking Time: 8 Minutes

Ingredients:
- 2 cups Brussels sprouts, halved
- 1 tablespoon balsamic vinegar
- 4 tablespoons olive oil
- Salt and pepper to taste

Directions:
1. Place a saucepan on medium-high fire and heat oil for a minute.
2. Add all ingredients and sauté for 7 minutes.
3. Season with pepper and salt.
4. Serve and enjoy.

Nutrition Info:
- Per Servings 4.6g Carbs, 1.5g Protein, 16.8g Fat, 162 Calories

Simple Tender Crisp Cauli-bites

Servings: 3 | Cooking Time: 10 Minutes

Ingredients:
- 2 cups cauliflower florets
- 2 clove garlic minced
- 4 tablespoons olive oil
- ¼ tsp salt
- ½ tsp pepper

Directions:
1. In a small bowl, mix well olive oil salt, pepper, and garlic.
2. Place cauliflower florets on a baking pan. Drizzle with seasoned oil and toss well to coat.
3. Evenly spread in a single layer and place a pan on the top rack of the oven.
4. Broil on low for 5 minutes. Turnover florets and return to the oven.
5. Continue cooking for another 5 minutes.
6. Serve and enjoy.

Nutrition Info:
- Per Servings 4.9g Carbs, 1.7g Protein, 18g Fat, 183 Calories

Cocktail Kielbasa With Mustard Sauce

Servings: 8 | Cooking Time: 6 Hours

Ingredients:
- 2 pounds kielbasa (Polish sausage)
- 1 jar prepared mustard
- 1 bay leaf
- Pepper to taste

Directions:
1. Slice kielbasa into bite-sized pieces.
2. Place all ingredients in the slow cooker.
3. Give a good stir to combine everything.
4. Close the lid and cook on low for 6 hours.
5. Remove the bay leaf.
6. Serve on toothpicks.

Nutrition Info:
- Per Servings 4g Carbs, 14g Protein, 20g Fat, 256 Calories

Boiled Stuffed Eggs

Servings: 6 | Cooking Time: 30 Minutes

Ingredients:
- 6 eggs
- 1 tbsp green tabasco
- ⅓ cup mayonnaise
- Salt to taste

Directions:
1. Place the eggs in a saucepan and cover with salted water. Bring to a boil over medium heat. Boil for 10 minutes. Place the eggs in an ice bath and let cool for 10 minutes.
2. Peel and slice in half lengthwise. Scoop out the yolks to a bowl; mash with a fork. Whisk together the tabasco, mayonnaise, mashed yolks, and salt, in a bowl. Spoon this mixture into egg white.

Nutrition Info:
- Per Servings 5g Carbs, 6g Protein, 17g Fat, 178 Calories

Basil Keto Crackers

Servings: 6 | Cooking Time: 15 Minutes

Ingredients:
- 1 ¼ cups almond flour
- ½ teaspoon baking powder
- ¼ teaspoon dried basil powder
- A pinch of cayenne pepper powder
- 1 clove of garlic, minced
- What you'll need from the store cupboard:
- Salt and pepper to taste
- 3 tablespoons oil

Directions:
1. Preheat oven to 350oF and lightly grease a cookie sheet with cooking spray.
2. Mix everything in a mixing bowl to create a dough.
3. Transfer the dough on a clean and flat working surface and spread out until 2mm thick. Cut into squares.
4. Place gently in an even layer on the prepped cookie sheet. Cook for 10 minutes.
5. Cook in batches.
6. Serve and enjoy.

Nutrition Info:
- Per Servings 2.9g Carbs, 5.3g Protein, 19.3g Fat, 205 Calories

Roasted String Beans, Mushrooms & Tomato Plate

Servings: 4 | Cooking Time: 32 Minutes

Ingredients:
- 2 cups strings beans, cut in halves
- 1 lb cremini mushrooms, quartered
- 3 tomatoes, quartered
- 2 cloves garlic, minced
- 3 tbsp olive oil
- 3 shallots, julienned
- ½ tsp dried thyme
- Salt and black pepper to season

Directions:

1. Preheat oven to 450ºF. In a bowl, mix the strings beans, mushrooms, tomatoes, garlic, olive oil, shallots, thyme, salt, and pepper. Pour the vegetables in a baking sheet and spread them all around.
2. Place the baking sheet in the oven and bake the veggies for 20 to 25 minutes.

Nutrition Info:
- Per Servings 6g Carbs, 6g Protein, 2g Fat, 121 Calories

Garlicky Cheddar Biscuits

Servings: 4 | Cooking Time: 20 Minutes

Ingredients:
- ⅓ cup almond flour
- 2 tsp garlic powder
- Salt to taste
- 1 tsp low carb baking powder
- 5 eggs
- ⅓ cup butter, melted
- 1 ¼ cup grated sharp cheddar cheese
- ⅓ cup Greek yogurt

Directions:

1. Preheat the oven to 350ºF. Mix the flour, garlic powder, salt, baking powder, and cheddar, in a bowl.
2. In a separate bowl, whisk the eggs, butter, and Greek yogurt, and then pour the resulting mixture into the dry ingredients. Stir well until a dough-like consistency has formed.
3. Fetch half soupspoons of the mixture onto a baking sheet with 2-inch intervals between each batter. Bake them in the oven for 12 minutes to be golden brown and remove them after. Serve.

Nutrition Info:
- Per Servings 1.4g Carbs, 5.4g Protein, 14.2g Fat, 153 Calories

Dill Pickles With Tuna-mayo Topping

Servings: 12 | Cooking Time: 40 Minutes

Ingredients:
- 18 ounces canned and drained tuna
- 6 large dill pickles
- ¼ tsp garlic powder
- ⅓ cup sugar-free mayonnaise
- 1 tbsp onion flakes

Directions:
1. Combine the mayonnaise, tuna, onion flakes, and garlic powder in a bowl. Cut the pickles in half lengthwise. Top each half with tuna mixture. Place in the fridge for 30 minutes before serving.

Nutrition Info:
- Per Servings 1.5g Carbs, 11g Protein, 10g Fat, 118 Calories

Cheesy Cheddar Cauliflower

Servings: 6 | Cooking Time: 20 Minutes

Ingredients:
- ½ cup butter
- 2 cups half and half cream
- 4 cups cheddar cheese, grated
- 3 cups cauliflower florets
- ½ cup water
- Pepper and salt to taste

Directions:
1. In a heavy-bottomed pot on medium-high fire, melt butter.
2. Stir in cream and cheddar cheese. Add in water. Mix well and cook for 5 minutes.
3. Add cauliflower florets and cook for 6 minutes. Season with pepper.
4. Serve and enjoy.

Nutrition Info:
- Per Servings 9g Carbs, 21g Protein, 42g Fat, 500 Calories

Chapter 3:
Poultry Recipes

Turkey Burgers With Fried Brussels Sprouts

Servings: 4 | Cooking Time: 30 Minutes

Ingredients:
- For the burgers
- 1 pound ground turkey
- 1 free-range egg
- ½ onion, chopped
- 1 tsp salt
- ½ tsp ground black pepper
- 1 tsp dried thyme
- 2 oz butter
- For the fried Brussels sprouts
- 1 ½ lb Brussels sprouts, halved
- 3 oz butter
- 1 tsp salt
- ½ tsp ground black pepper

Directions:
1. Combine the burger ingredients in a mixing bowl. Create patties from the mixture. Set a large pan over medium-high heat, warm butter, and fry the patties until cooked completely.
2. Place on a plate and cover with aluminium foil to keep warm. Fry brussels sprouts in butter, season to your preference, then set to a bowl. Plate the burgers and brussels sprouts and serve.

Nutrition Info:
- Per Servings 5.8g Carbs, 31g Protein, 25g Fat, 443 Calories

Chicken Pesto

Servings: 8 | Cooking Time: 35 Minutes

Ingredients:
- 5 cloves of garlic
- 4 skinless, boneless chicken breast halves, cut into thin strips
- 3 tbsp grated Parmesan cheese
- ¼ cup pesto
- 1 ¼ cups heavy cream
- 10 tbsps olive oil
- Pepper to taste
- 1/8 tsp salt

Directions:
1. On medium fire, place a large saucepan and heat olive oil.
2. Add garlic and chicken, sauté for 7 minutes, or until chicken strips are nearly cooked.
3. Lower fire and add Parmesan cheese, pesto, cream, pepper, and salt.
4. Continue cooking for 5-10 minutes more or until chicken is fully cooked. Stir frequently.
5. Once penne is cooked, drain well and pour into a large saucepan, toss to coat, and serve.

Nutrition Info:
- Per Servings 3g Carbs, 30.0g Protein, 22.0g Fat, 330 Calories

Spinach Artichoke Heart Chicken

Servings: 4 | Cooking Time: 30 Minutes

Ingredients:
- 4 chicken breasts
- 1 package frozen spinach
- 1 package cream cheese, softened
- ½ can quartered artichoke hearts, drained and chopped
- ¼ cup. shredded Parmesan cheese
- ¼ cup. mayonnaise
- 2 tbsp. olive oil
- 2 tbsps. grated mozzarella cheese
- ½ teaspoon. garlic powder
- Salt to taste

Directions:
1. Place the spinach in a bowl and microwave for 2 to 3 minutes. Let chill and drain.
2. Stir in cream cheese, artichoke hearts, Parmesan cheese, mayonnaise, garlic powder, and salt, whisk together. Cut chicken breasts to an even thickness. Spread salt and pepper over chicken breasts per side.
3. Preheat oven to 375 degrees F.
4. In a large skillet over medium-high, heat olive oil for 2 to 3 minutes. Lay chicken breasts in a large baking dish, pour spinach-artichoke mixture over chicken breasts. Place in the oven and bake at least 165 degrees F.
5. Sprinkle with mozzarella cheese and bake for 1 to 2 minutes more. Serve and enjoy.

Nutrition Info:
- Per Servings 5.4g Carbs, 56g Protein, 33.3g Fat, 554 Calories

Spinach Chicken Cheesy Bake

Servings: 6 | Cooking Time: 45 Minutes

Ingredients:
- 6 chicken breasts, skinless and boneless
- 1 tsp mixed spice seasoning
- Pink salt and black pepper to season
- 2 loose cups baby spinach
- 3 tsp olive oil
- 4 oz cream cheese, cubed
- 1 ¼ cups shredded mozzarella cheese
- 4 tbsp water

Directions:
1. Preheat oven to 370ºF.
2. Season chicken with spice mix, salt, and black pepper. Pat with your hands to have the seasoning stick on the chicken. Put in the casserole dish and layer spinach over the chicken. Mix the oil with cream cheese, mozzarella, salt, and black pepper and stir in water a tablespoon at a time. Pour the mixture over the chicken and cover the pot with aluminium foil.
3. Bake for 20 minutes, remove foil and continue cooking for 15 minutes until a nice golden brown color is formed on top. Take out and allow sitting for 5 minutes.
4. Serve warm with braised asparagus.

Nutrition Info:
- Per Servings 3.1g Carbs, 15g Protein, 30.2g Fat, 340 Calories

Turkey Breast Salad

Servings: 4 | Cooking Time: 25 Minutes

Ingredients:
- 1 tbsp swerve
- 1 red onion, chopped
- ¼ cup vinegar
- ¼ cup olive oil
- ¼ cup water
- 1¾ cups raspberries
- 1 tbsp Dijon mustard
- Salt and ground black pepper, to taste
- 10 ounces baby spinach
- 2 medium turkey breasts, boneless
- 4 ounces goat cheese, crumbled
- ½ cup pecans halves

Directions:
1. Using a blender, combine swerve, vinegar, 1 cup raspberries, pepper, mustard, water, onion, oil, and salt, and ensure well blended. Strain this into a bowl, and set aside. Cut the turkey breast in half, add a seasoning of pepper and salt, and place skin side down into a pan.
2. Cook for 8 minutes flipping to the other side and cooking for 5 minutes. Split the spinach among plates, spread with the remaining raspberries, pecan halves, and goat cheese. Slice the turkey breasts, put over the salad and top with raspberries vinaigrette and enjoy.

Nutrition Info:
- Per Servings 6g Carbs, 28g Protein, 33g Fat, 451 Calories

Creamy Stuffed Chicken With Parma Ham

Servings: 4 | Cooking Time: 40 Minutes

Ingredients:
- 4 chicken breasts
- 2 tbsp olive oil
- 3 cloves garlic, minced
- 3 shallots, finely chopped
- 4 tbsp dried mixed herbs
- 8 slices Parma ham
- 8 oz cream cheese
- 2 lemons, zested
- Salt and black pepper to taste

Directions:
1. Preheat the oven to 350ºF.
2. Heat the oil in a small skillet and sauté the garlic and shallots with a pinch of salt and lemon zest for 3 minutes. Turn the heat off and let it cool. After, stir the cream cheese and mixed herbs into the shallot mixture.
3. Score a pocket in each chicken breast, fill the holes with the cream cheese mixture and cover with the cut-out chicken. Wrap each breast with two Parma ham and secure the ends with a toothpick.
4. Lay the chicken parcels on a greased baking sheet and cook in the oven for 20 minutes. After cooking, remove to rest for 4 minutes before serving with a green salad and roasted tomatoes.

Nutrition Info:
- Per Scrvings 2g Carbs, 26g Protein, 35g Fat, 485 Calories

Stewed Chicken Salsa

Servings: 4 | Cooking Time: 25 Minutes

Ingredients:
- 1 cup shredded cheddar cheese
- 8-ounces cream cheese
- 16-ounces salsa
- 4 skinless and boneless thawed chicken breasts
- 4 tablespoons butter
- 1 cup water

Directions:
1. Add all ingredients in a pot, except for sour cream, on high fire, and bring to a boil.
2. Once boiling, lower fire to a simmer and cook for 20 minutes.
3. Adjust seasoning to taste and stir in sour cream.
4. Serve and enjoy.

Nutrition Info:
- Per Servings 9.6g Carbs, 67.8g Protein, 32.6g Fat, 658 Calories

Rosemary Grilled Chicken

Servings: 4 | Cooking Time: 12 Minutes

Ingredients:
- 1 tablespoon fresh parsley, finely chopped
- 1 tablespoon fresh rosemary, finely chopped
- 4 tablespoons olive oil
- 4 pieces of 4-oz chicken breast, boneless and skinless
- 5 cloves garlic, minced
- Pepper and salt to taste

Directions:
1. In a shallow and large bowl, mix salt, parsley, rosemary, olive oil, and garlic. Place chicken breast and marinate in the bowl of herbs for at least an hour or more before grilling.
2. Grease grill, grate and preheat grill to medium-high fire. Once hot, grill chicken for 4 to 5 minutes per side or until juices run a clear and internal temperature of chicken is 168oF.

Nutrition Info:
- Per Servings 1.0g Carbs, 34.0g Protein, 16.0g Fat, 238 Calories

Garlic & Ginger Chicken With Peanut Sauce

Servings: 6 | Cooking Time: 1 Hour And 50 Minutes

Ingredients:
- 1 tbsp wheat-free soy sauce
- 1 tbsp sugar-free fish sauce
- 1 tbsp lime juice
- 1 tsp cilantro
- 1 tsp minced garlic
- 1 tsp minced ginger
- 1 tbsp olive oil
- 1 tbsp rice wine vinegar
- 1 tsp cayenne pepper
- 1 tsp erythritol
- 6 chicken thighs
- Sauce:
- ½ cup peanut butter
- 1 tsp minced garlic
- 1 tbsp lime juice
- 2 tbsp water
- 1 tsp minced ginger
- 1 tbsp chopped jalapeño
- 2 tbsp rice wine vinegar
- 2 tbsp erythritol
- 1 tbsp fish sauce

Directions:
1. Combine all chicken ingredients in a large Ziploc bag. Seal the bag and shake to combine. Refrigerate for 1 hour. Remove from fridge about 15 minutes before cooking.
2. Preheat the grill to medium and grill the chicken for 7 minutes per side. Whisk together all sauce ingredients in a mixing bowl. Serve the chicken drizzled with peanut sauce.

Nutrition Info:
- Per Servings 3g Carbs, 35g Protein, 36g Fat, 492 Calories

Lemon & Rosemary Chicken In A Skillet

Servings: 4 | Cooking Time: 1 Hour And 20 Minutes

Ingredients:
- 8 chicken thighs
- 1 tsp salt
- 2 tbsp lemon juice
- 1 tsp lemon zest
- 2 tbsp olive oil
- 1 tbsp chopped rosemary
- ¼ tsp black pepper
- 1 garlic clove, minced

Directions:
1. Combine all ingredients in a bowl. Place in the fridge for one hour.
2. Heat a skillet over medium heat. Add the chicken along with the juices and cook until crispy, about 7 minutes per side.

Nutrition Info:
- Per Servings 2.5g Carbs, 31g Protein, 31g Fat, 477 Calories

Parmesan Wings With Yogurt Sauce

Servings: 6 | Cooking Time: 25 Minutes

Ingredients:
- For the Dipping Sauce
- 1 cup plain yogurt
- 1 tsp fresh lemon juice
- Salt and black pepper to taste
- For the Wings
- 2 lb chicken wings
- Salt and black pepper to taste
- Cooking spray
- ½ cup melted butter
- ½ cup Hot sauce
- ¼ cup grated Parmesan cheese

Directions:
1. Mix the yogurt, lemon juice, salt, and black pepper in a bowl. Chill while making the chicken.
2. Preheat oven to 400°F and season wings with salt and black pepper. Line them on a baking sheet and grease lightly with cooking spray. Bake for 20 minutes until golden brown. Mix butter, hot sauce, and parmesan in a bowl. Toss chicken in the sauce to evenly coat and plate. Serve with yogurt dipping sauce and celery strips.

Nutrition Info:
- Per Servings 4g Carbs, 24g Protein, 36.4g Fat, 452 Calories

Slow Cooked Chicken Drumstick

Servings: 12 | Cooking Time: 7 Hours

Ingredients:
- 12 chicken drumsticks
- 1 ½ tbsp paprika
- ¼ tsp dried thyme
- ½ tsp onion powder
- 2 tbsp Worcestershire sauce
- Salt and pepper to taste
- ½ cup water

Directions:
1. Place all ingredients in the slow cooker. Give a good stir to coat the entire chicken with the spices.
2. Close the slow cooker, press high settings, and cook for 7 hours.
3. Serve and enjoy.

Nutrition Info:
- Per Servings 2.5g Carbs, 23.8g Protein, 12.1g Fat, 218 Calories

Stuffed Chicken Breasts With Cucumber Noodle Salad

Servings: 4 | Cooking Time: 60 Minutes

Ingredients:
- For the chicken
- 4 chicken breasts
- 1/3 cup baby spinach
- 1/4 cup goat cheese
- 1/4 cup shredded cheddar cheese
- 4 tbsp butter
- Salt and black pepper, to taste
- For the tomato sauce
- 1 tbsp butter
- 1 shallot, chopped
- 2 garlic cloves, chopped
- ½ tbsp red wine vinegar
- 2 tbsp tomato paste
- 14 oz canned crushed tomatoes
- ½ tsp salt
- 1 tsp dried basil
- 1 tsp dried oregano
- Black pepper, to taste
- For the salad
- 2 cucumbers, spiralized
- 2 tbsp olive oil
- 1 tbsp rice vinegar

Directions:
1. Set oven to 400ºF and grease a baking dish. Set aside.
2. Place a pan over medium heat. Melt 2 tbsp of butter and sauté spinach until it shrinks; season with salt and pepper. Transfer into a medium bowl containing the goat cheese, stir and set to one side. Cut the chicken breasts lengthwise and stuff with the cheese mixture and set into the baking dish. On top, spread the grated cheddar cheese, add 2 tbsp of butter then set into the oven. Bake until cooked through for 20-30 minutes.
3. Set a pan over medium-high heat and warm 1 tbsp of butter. Add in garlic and shallot and cook until soft. Place in herbs, tomato paste, vinegar, tomatoes, salt, and pepper. Bring the mixture to a boil. Set heat to low and simmer for 15 minutes.
4. Arrange the cucumbers on a serving platter, season with salt, pepper, olive oil, and vinegar, Top with the chicken and pour over the sauce.

Nutrition Info:
- Per Servings 6g Carbs, 43g Protein, 31g Fat, 453 Calories

Zesty Grilled Chicken

Servings: 8 | Cooking Time: 35 Minutes

Ingredients:
- 2½ pounds chicken thighs and drumsticks
- 1 tbsp coconut aminos
- 1 tbsp apple cider vinegar
- A pinch of red pepper flakes
- Salt and black pepper, to taste
- ½ tsp ground ginger
- ⅓ cup butter
- 1 garlic clove, minced
- 1 tsp lime zest
- ½ cup warm water

Directions:
1. In a blender, combine the butter with water, salt, ginger, vinegar, garlic, pepper, lime zest, aminos, and pepper flakes. Pat the chicken pieces dry, lay on a pan, and top with the zesty marinade.
2. Toss to coat and refrigerate for 1 hour. Set the chicken pieces skin side down on a preheated grill over medium-high heat, cook for 10 minutes, turn, brush with some marinade, and cook for 10 minutes. Split among serving plates and enjoy.

Nutrition Info:
- Per Servings 3g Carbs, 42g Protein, 12g Fat, 375 Calories

Heart Healthy Chicken Salad

Servings: 4 | Cooking Time: 45 Minutes

Ingredients:
- 3 tbsp mayonnaise, low-fat
- ½ tsp onion powder
- 1 tbsp lemon juice
- ¼ cup celery (chopped)
- 3 ¼ cups chicken breast (cooked, cubed, and skinless)
- Salt and pepper to taste

Directions:
1. Bake chicken breasts for 45 minutes at 350oF. Let it cool and cut them into cubes and place them in the refrigerator.
2. Combine all other ingredients in a large bowl then add the chilled chicken.
3. Mix well and ready to serve.
4. Enjoy!

Nutrition Info:
- Per Servings 1.0g Carbs, 50.0g Protein, 22.0g Fat, 408 Calories

Chicken With Anchovy Tapenade

Servings: 2 | Cooking Time: 30 Minutes

Ingredients:
- 1 chicken breast, cut into 4 pieces
- 2 tbsp coconut oil
- 3 garlic cloves, and crushed
- For the tapenade
- 1 cup black olives, pitted
- 1 oz anchovy fillets, rinsed
- 1 garlic clove, crushed
- Salt and ground black pepper, to taste
- 2 tbsp olive oil
- ¼ cup fresh basil, chopped
- 1 tbsp lemon juice

Directions:
1. Using a food processor, combine the olives, salt, olive oil, basil, lemon juice, anchovy fillets, and pepper, blend well. Set a pan over medium-high heat and warm coconut oil, stir in the garlic, and cook for 2 minutes.
2. Place in the chicken pieces and cook each side for 4 minutes. Split the chicken among plates and apply a topping of the anchovy tapenade.

Nutrition Info:
- Per Servings 3g Carbs, 25g Protein, 13g Fat, 155 Calories

Chicken Cacciatore

Servings: 6 | Cooking Time: 35 Minutes

Ingredients:
- 6 chicken drumsticks, bone-in
- 1 bay leaf
- 4 roma tomatoes, chopped
- ½ cup black olives, pitted
- 3 cloves garlic, minced
- Salt and pepper to taste
- 1 cup water
- 1 tsp oil

Directions:
1. On high fire, heat a saucepan for 2 minutes. Add oil to the pan and swirl to coat bottom and sides. Heat oil for a minute.
2. Add garlic and sauté for a minute. Stir in tomatoes and bay leaf. Crumble and wilt tomatoes for 5 minutes.
3. Add chicken and continue sautéing for 7 minutes.
4. Deglaze the pot with ½ cup water.
5. Add remaining ingredients. Season generously with salt and pepper.
6. Lower fire to low, cover, and simmer for 20 minutes.
7. Serve and enjoy.

Nutrition Info:
- Per Servings 9.5g Carbs, 25.3g Protein, 13.2g Fat, 256 Calories

Roast Chicken With Herb Stuffing

Servings: 8 | Cooking Time: 120 Minutes

Ingredients:
- 5-pound whole chicken
- 1 bunch oregano
- 1 bunch thyme
- 1 tbsp marjoram
- 1 tbsp parsley
- 1 tbsp olive oil
- 2 pounds Brussels sprouts
- 1 lemon
- 4 tbsp butter

Directions:
1. Preheat your oven to 450ºF.
2. Stuff the chicken with oregano, thyme, and lemon. Make sure the wings are tucked over and behind.
3. Roast for 15 minutes. Reduce the heat to 325ºF and cook for 40 minutes. Spread the butter over the chicken, and sprinkle parsley and marjoram. Add the brussels sprouts. Return to the oven and bake for 40 more minutes. Let sit for 10 minutes before carving.

Nutrition Info:
- Per Servings 5.1g Carbs, 30g Protein, 32g Fat, 432 Calories

Chicken And Mushrooms

Servings: 8 | Cooking Time: 15 Minutes

Ingredients:
- 1 large shallot, diced
- 8 chicken breasts, cubed
- 4 large cremini mushrooms, sliced
- ¼ cup yogurt
- 5 tablespoons olive oil
- ½ cup water
- Salt and pepper to taste

Directions:
1. Heat oil in a skillet over medium flame and sauté the shallot until fragrant.
2. Stir in the chicken breasts and continue cooking for 3 minutes while stirring constantly.
3. Add the mushrooms, water, and yogurt.
4. Season with salt and pepper to taste.
5. Close the lid and bring to a boil.
6. Reduce the heat to medium-low and allow simmering for 10 minutes.

Nutrition Info:
- Per Servings 1.5g Carbs, 55.8g Protein, 27.7g Fat, 512 Calories

Chicken In Creamy Spinach Sauce

Servings: 4 | Cooking Time: 20 Minutes

Ingredients:
- 1 pound chicken thighs
- 2 tbsp coconut oil
- 2 tbsp coconut flour
- 2 cups spinach, chopped
- 1 tsp oregano
- 1 cup heavy cream
- 1 cup chicken broth
- 2 tbsp butter

Directions:
1. Warm the coconut oil in a skillet and brown the chicken on all sides, about 6-8 minutes. Set aside.
2. Melt the butter and whisk in the flour over medium heat. Whisk in the heavy cream and chicken broth and bring to a boil. Stir in oregano. Add the spinach to the skillet and cook until wilted.
3. Add the thighs in the skillet and cook for an additional 5 minutes.

Nutrition Info:
- Per Servings 2.6g Carbs, 18g Protein, 38g Fat, 446 Calories

Pancetta & Chicken Casserole

Servings: 3 | Cooking Time: 40 Minutes

Ingredients:
- 8 pancetta strips, chopped
- ⅓ cup Dijon mustard
- Salt and black pepper, to taste
- 1 onion, chopped
- 1 tbsp olive oil
- 1½ cups chicken stock
- 3 chicken breasts, skinless and boneless
- ¼ tsp sweet paprika

Directions:

1. Using a bowl, combine the paprika, pepper, salt, and mustard. Sprinkle this on chicken breasts and massage. Set a pan over medium-high heat, stir in the pancetta, cook until it browns, and remove to a plate. Place oil in the same pan and heat over medium-high heat, add in the chicken breasts, cook for each side for 2 minutes and set aside.

2. Place in the stock, and bring to a simmer. Stir in pepper, pancetta, salt, and onion. Return the chicken to the pan as well, stir gently, and simmer for 20 minutes over medium heat, turning the meat halfway through. Split the chicken on serving plates, sprinkle the sauce over it to serve.

Nutrition Info:
- Per Servings 3g Carbs, 26g Protein, 18g Fat, 313 Calories

One Pot Chicken With Mushrooms

Servings: 6 | Cooking Time: 35 Minutes

Ingredients:
- 2 cups sliced mushrooms
- ½ tsp onion powder
- ½ tsp garlic powder
- ¼ cup butter
- 1 tsp Dijon mustard
- 1 tbsp tarragon, chopped
- 2 pounds chicken thighs
- Salt and black pepper, to taste

Directions:

1. Season the thighs with salt, pepper, garlic, and onion powder. Melt the butter in a skillet, and cook the chicken until browned; set aside. Add mushrooms to the same fat and cook for about 5 minutes.

2. Stir in Dijon mustard and ½ cup of water. Return the chicken to the skillet. Season to taste with salt and pepper, reduce the heat and cover, and let simmer for 15 minutes. Stir in tarragon. Serve warm.

Nutrition Info:
- Per Servings 1g Carbs, 31g Protein, 37g Fat, 447 Calories

Rosemary Turkey Pie

Servings: 4 | Cooking Time: 40 Minutes

Ingredients:
- 2 cups chicken stock
- 1 cup turkey meat, cooked and chopped
- Salt and ground black pepper, to taste
- 1 tsp fresh rosemary, chopped
- ½ cup kale, chopped
- ½ cup butternut squash, chopped
- ½ cup Monterey jack cheese, shredded
- ¼ tsp smoked paprika
- ¼ tsp garlic powder
- ¼ tsp xanthan gum
- Cooking spray
- For the crust:
- ¼ cup butter
- ¼ tsp xanthan gum
- 2 cups almond flour
- A pinch of salt
- 1 egg
- ¼ cup cheddar cheese

Directions:

1. Set a greased pot over medium-high heat. Place in turkey and squash, and cook for 10 minutes. Stir in stock, Monterey Jack cheese, garlic powder, rosemary, pepper, smoked paprika, kale, and salt.

2. In a bowl, combine ½ cup stock from the pot with ¼ teaspoon xanthan gum, and transfer everything to the pot; set aside. In a separate bowl, stir together salt, ¼ teaspoon xanthan gum, and flour.

3. Stir in the butter, cheddar cheese, egg, until a pie crust dough forms. Form into a ball and refrigerate. Spray a baking dish with cooking spray and sprinkle pie filling on the bottom. Set the dough on a working surface, roll into a circle, and top filling with this. Ensure well pressed and seal edges, set in an oven at 350ºF, and bake for 35 minutes. Allow the pie to cool, and enjoy.

Nutrition Info:
- Per Servings 5.6g Carbs, 21g Protein, 23g Fat, 325 Calories

Chicken And Bacon Rolls

Servings: 4 | Cooking Time: 45 Minutes

Ingredients:
- 1 tbsp fresh chives, chopped
- 8 ounces blue cheese
- 2 pounds chicken breasts, skinless, boneless, halved
- 12 bacon slices
- 2 tomatoes, chopped
- Salt and ground black pepper, to taste

Directions:

1. Set a pan over medium heat, place in the bacon, cook until halfway done, remove to paper towels, and drain the grease. Using a bowl, stir together the blue cheese, chives, tomatoes, pepper, and salt.

2. Use a meat tenderizer to flatten the chicken breasts well, season and lay the cream cheese mixture on top. Roll them up, and wrap each in a bacon slice. Place the wrapped chicken breasts in a greased baking dish, and roast in the oven at 370ºF for 30 minutes. Serve on top of wilted kale.

Nutrition Info:
- Per Servings 5g Carbs, 38g Protein, 48g Fat, 623 Calories

Turkey & Mushroom Bake

Servings: 8 | Cooking Time: 55 Minutes

Ingredients:
- 4 cups mushrooms, sliced
- 1 egg, whisked
- 3 cups green cabbage, shredded
- 3 cups turkey meat, cooked and chopped
- ½ cup chicken stock
- ½ cup cream cheese
- 1 tsp poultry seasoning
- 2 cup cheddar cheese, grated
- ½ cup Parmesan cheese, grated
- Salt and ground black pepper, to taste
- ¼ tsp garlic powder

Directions:

1. Set a pan over medium-low heat. Stir in chicken broth, egg, Parmesan cheese, pepper, garlic powder, poultry seasoning, cheddar cheese, cream cheese, and salt, and simmer.

2. Place in the cabbage and turkey meat, and set away from the heat.

3. Add the mushrooms, pepper, turkey mixture and salt in a baking dish and spread. Place aluminum foil to cover, set in an oven at 390ºF, and bake for 35 minutes. Allow cooling and enjoy.

Nutrition Info:
- Per Servings 3g Carbs, 25g Protein, 15g Fat, 245 Calories

Chapter 4: Fish And Seafood Recipes

Smoked Mackerel Patties

Servings: 6 | Cooking Time: 30 Minutes

Ingredients:
- 1 turnip, peeled and diced
- 1 ½ cup water
- Pink salt and chili pepper to taste
- 3 tbsp olive oil + for rubbing
- 4 smoked mackerel steaks, bones removed, flaked
- 3 eggs, beaten
- 2 tbsp mayonnaise
- 1 tbsp pork rinds, crushed

Directions:

1. Bring the turnip to boil in salted water in a saucepan over medium heat for 8 minutes or until tender. Drain the turnip through a colander, transfer to a mixing bowl, and mash the lumps.

2. Add the mackerel, eggs, mayonnaise, pork rinds, salt, and chili pepper. With gloves on your hands, mix and make 6 compact patties.

3. Heat olive oil in a skillet over medium heat and fry the patties for 3 minutes on each side to be golden brown. Remove onto a wire rack to cool. Serve with sesame lime dipping sauce.

Nutrition Info:
- Per Servings 2.2g Carbs, 16g Protein, 27.1g Fat, 324 Calories

Red Cabbage Tilapia Taco Bowl

Servings: 4 | Cooking Time: 20 Minutes

Ingredients:
- 2 cups cauli rice
- Water for sprinkling
- 2 tsp ghee
- 4 tilapia fillets, cut into cubes
- ¼ tsp taco seasoning
- Pink salt and chili pepper to taste
- ¼ head red cabbage, shredded
- 1 ripe avocado, pitted and chopped

Directions:

1. Sprinkle cauli rice in a bowl with a little water and microwave for 3 minutes. Fluff after with a fork and set aside. Melt ghee in a skillet over medium heat, rub the tilapia with the taco seasoning, salt, and chili pepper, and fry until brown on all sides, for about 8 minutes in total.

2. Transfer to a plate and set aside. In 4 serving bowls, share the cauli rice, cabbage, fish, and avocado. Serve with chipotle lime sour cream dressing.

Nutrition Info:
- Per Servings 4g Carbs, 16.5g Protein, 23.4g Fat, 269 Calories

Salmon And Cauliflower Rice Pilaf

Servings: 4 | Cooking Time: 25 Minutes

Ingredients:
- 1 cauliflower head, shredded
- ¼ cup dried vegetable soup mix
- 1 cup chicken broth
- 1 pinch saffron
- 1-lb wild salmon fillets
- 6 tbsp olive oil
- Pepper and salt to taste

Directions:
1. Place a heavy-bottomed pot on medium-high fire and add all ingredients and mix well.
2. Bring to a boil, lower fire to a simmer, and simmer for 10 minutes.
3. Turn off fire, shred salmon, adjust seasoning to taste.
4. Let it rest for 5 minutes.
5. Fluff again, serve, and enjoy.

Nutrition Info:
- Per Servings 4.7g Carbs, 31.8g Protein, 31.5g Fat, 429 Calories

Chipotle Salmon Asparagus

Servings: 2 | Cooking Time: 15 Minutes

Ingredients:
- 1-lb salmon fillet, skin on
- 2 teaspoon chipotle paste
- A handful of asparagus spears, trimmed
- 1 lemon, sliced thinly
- A pinch of rosemary
- Salt to taste
- 5 tbsp olive oil

Directions:
1. In a heat-proof dish that fits inside the saucepan, add asparagus spears on the bottom of the dish. Place fish, top with rosemary, and lemon slices. Season with chipotle paste and salt. Drizzle with olive oil. Cover dish with foil.
2. Place a large saucepan on the medium-high fire. Place a trivet inside the saucepan and fill the pan halfway with water. Cover and bring to a boil.
3. Place dish on the trivet.
4. Cover pan and steam for 10 minutes. Let it rest in pan for another 5 minutes.
5. Serve and enjoy topped with pepper.

Nutrition Info:
- Per Servings 2.8g Carbs, 35.0g Protein, 50.7g Fat, 651 Calories

Tuna Steaks With Shirataki Noodles

Servings: 4 | Cooking Time: 30 Minutes

Ingredients:
- 1 pack miracle noodle angel hair
- 3 cups water
- Cooking spray
- 1 red bell pepper, seeded and halved
- 4 tuna steaks
- Salt and black pepper to taste
- Olive oil for brushing
- 2 tbsp pickled ginger
- 2 tbsp chopped cilantro

Directions:

1. Cook the shirataki rice as per package instructions: In a colander, rinse the shirataki noodles with running cold water. Bring a pot of salted water to a boil; blanch the noodles for 2 minutes. Drain and transfer to a dry skillet over medium heat. Dry roast for a minute until opaque.

2. Grease a grill's grate with cooking spray and preheat on medium heat. Season the red bell pepper and tuna with salt and black pepper, brush with olive oil, and grill covered. Cook both for 3 minutes on each side. Transfer to a plate to cool. Dice bell pepper with a knife.

3. Assemble the noodles, tuna, and bell pepper in serving plate. Top with pickled ginger and garnish with cilantro. Serve with roasted sesame sauce (low-carb).

Nutrition Info:
- Per Servings 2g Carbs, 22g Protein, 18.2g Fat, 310 Calories

Chili-lime Shrimps

Servings: 4 | Cooking Time: 10 Minutes

Ingredients:
- 1 ½ lb. raw shrimp, peeled and deveined
- 1 tbsp. chili flakes
- 5 tbsp sweet chili sauce
- 2 tbsp. lime juice, freshly squeezed
- 1 tsp cayenne pepper
- Salt and pepper to taste
- 5 tbsp oil
- 3 tbsp water

Directions:

1. In a small bowl, whisk well chili flakes, sweet chili sauce, cayenne pepper, and water.
2. On medium-high fire, heat a nonstick saucepan for 2 minutes. Add oil to a pan and swirl to coat bottom and sides. Heat oil for a minute.
3. Stir fry shrimp, around 5 minutes. Season lightly with salt and pepper.
4. Stir in sweet chili mixture and toss well shrimp to coat.
5. Turn off fire, drizzle lime juice and toss well to coat.
6. Serve and enjoy.

Nutrition Info:
- Per Servings 1.7g Carbs, 34.9g Protein, 19.8g Fat, 306 Calories

Bacon Wrapped Salmon

Serves: 2 | Cooking Time: 15 Minutes

Ingredients:
- 2 6-ounces salmon fillets
- 2 streaky bacon slices
- 4 tablespoons pesto

Directions:
1. Preheat the oven to 350 °F and line a medium baking sheet with parchment paper.
2. Wrap each salmon fillet with 1 bacon slice and then, secure with a wooden skewer.
3. Place 2 tablespoons of pesto in the center of each salmon fillet.
4. Arrange the salmon fillets onto prepared baking sheet.
5. Bake for about 15 minutes.
6. Remove the salmon fillets from oven and transfer onto the serving plates.
7. Serve hot.

Nutrition Info:
- Per Serving: 1.9g Carbs; 46.7g Protein; 35.6g Fat; 57 Calories;

Sushi Shrimp Rolls

Servings: 5 | Cooking Time: 10 Minutes

Ingredients:
- 2 cups cooked and chopped shrimp
- 1 tbsp sriracha sauce
- ¼ cucumber, julienned
- 5 hand roll nori sheets
- ¼ cup mayonnaise

Directions:
1. Combine shrimp, mayonnaise, and sriracha in a bowl. Lay out a single nori sheet on a flat surface and spread about 1/5 of the shrimp mixture. Roll the nori sheet as desired. Repeat with the other ingredients. Serve with sugar-free soy sauce.

Nutrition Info:
- Per Servings 1g Carbs, 18.7g Protein, 10g Fat, 216 Calories

Asian-style Steamed Mussels

Serves:6 | Cooking Time: 25 Minutes

Ingredients:
- 5 tbsp sesame oil
- 1 onion, chopped
- 3 lb mussels, cleaned
- 2 garlic cloves, minced
- 12 oz coconut milk
- 16 oz white wine
- 1 lime, juiced
- 2 tsp red curry powder
- 2 tbsp cilantro, chopped

Directions:
1. Warm the sesame oil in a saucepan over medium heat and cook onion and garlic cloves for 3 minutes. Pour in wine, coconut milk, and curry powder and cook for 5 minutes. Add mussels, turn off the heat, cover the saucepan, and steam the mussels until the shells open up, 5 minutes. Discard any closed mussels. Top with cilantro and serve.

Nutrition Info:
- Per Serves 5.4g Carbs ; 28.2g Protein;16g Fat ; 323 Calories

Avocado Salad With Shrimp

Serves: 4 | Cooking Time:10 Minutes

Ingredients:
- 2 tomatoes, sliced into cubes
- 2 medium avocados, cut into large pieces
- 3 tablespoons red onion, diced
- ½ large lettuce, chopped
- 2 lbs. shrimp, peeled and deveined
- For the Lime Vinaigrette Dressing
- 2 cloves garlic, minced
- 1 ½ teaspoon Dijon mustard
- 1/3 cup extra virgin olive oil
- salt and pepper to taste
- 1/3 cup lime juice

Directions:
1. Add the peeled and deveined shrimp and 2 quarts of water to a cooking pot and print to a boil, lower the heat and let them simmer for 1-2 minutes until the shrimp is pink. Set aside and let them cool.
2. Next add the chopped lettuce in a large bowl. Then add the avocado, tomatoes, shrimp and red onion.
3. In a small bowl whisk together the Dijon mustard, garlic, olive oil and lime juice. Mix well.
4. Pour the lime vinaigrette dressing over the salad and serve.

Nutrition Info:
- Per serving: 7g Carbs; 43.5g Protein; 17.6g Fat; 377 Calories;

Cilantro Shrimp

Servings: 4 | Cooking Time: 10 Minutes

Ingredients:
- 1/2 cup reduced-fat Asian sesame salad dressing
- 1-pound uncooked shrimp, peeled and deveined
- Lime wedges
- 1/4 cup chopped fresh cilantro
- 5 tablespoon olive oil
- Salt and pepper

Directions:
1. In a large nonstick skillet, heat 1 tablespoon dressing over medium heat. Add shrimp; cook and stir 1 minute.
2. Stir in remaining dressing; cook, uncovered, until shrimp turn pink, 1-2 minutes longer.
3. To serve, squeeze lime juice over the top; sprinkle with cilantro, pepper, and salt. If desired, serve with rice.

Nutrition Info:
- Per Servings 4.7g Carbs, 32g Protein, 39g Fat, 509 Calories

Blue Cheese Shrimps

Servings: 6 | Cooking Time: 15 Minutes

Ingredients:
- 3 ounces cream cheese, softened
- 2/3 cup minced fresh parsley, divided
- 1/4 cup crumbled blue cheese
- 1/2 teaspoon Creole mustard
- 24 cooked jumbo shrimp, peeled and deveined
- Pepper and salt to taste
- 5 tablespoon olive oil

Directions:
1. In a small bowl, beat cream cheese until smooth. Beat in 1/3 cup parsley, blue cheese, and mustard. Season with pepper and salt as desired. Refrigerate at least 1 hour.
2. Make a deep slit along the back of each shrimp to within 1/4-1/2 inch of the bottom. Stuff with cream cheese mixture; press remaining parsley onto cream cheese mixture.
3. Drizzle with olive oil last.

Nutrition Info:
- Per Servings 1.7g Carbs, 6g Protein, 17.8g Fat, 180 Calories

Thyme-sesame Crusted Halibut

Servings: 2 | Cooking Time: 15 Minutes

Ingredients:
- 8 oz. halibut, cut into 2 portions
- 1 tbsp. lemon juice, freshly squeezed
- 1 tsp. dried thyme leaves
- 1 tbsp. sesame seeds, toasted
- Salt and pepper to taste

Directions:
1. Place a trivet in a large saucepan and pour a cup or two of water into the pan. Bring it to a boil.
2. Place halibut in a heatproof dish that fits inside a saucepan. Season with lemon juice, salt, and pepper. Sprinkle with dried thyme leaves and sesame seeds.
3. Seal dish with foil. Place the dish on the trivet inside the saucepan. Cover and steam for 15 minutes.
4. Serve and enjoy.

Nutrition Info:
- Per Servings 4.2g Carbs, 17.5g Protein, 17.7g Fat, 246 Calories

Grilled Shrimp With Chimichurri Sauce

Servings: 4 | Cooking Time: 55 Minutes

Ingredients:
- 1 pound shrimp, peeled and deveined
- 2 tbsp olive oil
- Juice of 1 lime
- Chimichurri
- ½ tsp salt
- ¼ cup olive oil
- 2 garlic cloves
- ¼ cup red onion, chopped
- ¼ cup red wine vinegar
- ½ tsp pepper
- 2 cups parsley
- ¼ tsp red pepper flakes

Directions:
1. Process the chimichurri ingredients in a blender until smooth; set aside. Combine shrimp, olive oil, and lime juice, in a bowl, and let marinate in the fridge for 30 minutes. Preheat your grill to medium. Add shrimp and cook about 2 minutes per side. Serve shrimp drizzled with the chimichurri sauce.

Nutrition Info:
- Per Servings 3.5g Carbs, 16g Protein, 20.3g Fat, 283 Calories

Buttery Almond Lemon Tilapia

Servings: 4 | Cooking Time: 10 Minutes

Ingredients:
- 4 tilapia fillets
- 1/4 cup butter, cubed
- 1/4 cup white wine or chicken broth
- 2 tablespoons lemon juice
- 1/4 cup sliced almonds
- 1/2 teaspoon salt
- 1/4 teaspoon pepper
- 1 tablespoon olive oil

Directions:
1. Sprinkle fillets with salt and pepper. In a large nonstick skillet, heat oil over medium heat.
2. Add fillets; cook until fish just begins to flake easily with a fork, 2-3 minutes on each side. Remove and keep warm.
3. Add butter, wine and lemon juice to the same pan; cook and stir until butter is melted.
4. Serve with fish; sprinkle with almonds.

Nutrition Info:
- Per Servings 2g Carbs, 22g Protein, 19g Fat, 269 Calories

Asian Seafood Stir-fry

Serves: 4 | Cooking Time: 15 Minutes

Ingredients:
- 4 teaspoons sesame oil
- 1/2 cup yellow onion, sliced
- 1 cup asparagus spears, sliced
- 1/2 cup celery, chopped
- 1/2 cup enoki mushrooms
- 1 pound bay scallops
- 1 tablespoon fresh parsley, chopped
- Kosher salt and ground black pepper, to taste
- 1/2 teaspoon red pepper flakes, crushed
- 1 tablespoon coconut aminos
- 2 tablespoons rice wine
- 1/2 cup dry roasted peanuts, roughly chopped

Directions:

1. Heat 1 teaspoon of the sesame oil in a wok over a medium-high flame. Now, fry the onion until crisp-tender and translucent; reserve.
2. Heat another teaspoon of the sesame oil and fry the asparagus and celery for about 3 minutes until crisp-tender; reserve.
3. Then, heat another teaspoon of the sesame oil and cook the mushrooms for 2 minutes more or until they start to soften; reserve.
4. Lastly, heat the remaining teaspoon of sesame oil and cook the bay scallops just until they are opaque.
5. Return all reserved vegetables to the wok. Add in the remaining ingredients and toss to combine. Serve warm and enjoy!

Nutrition Info:
- Per Serves 5.9g Carbs; 27g Protein; 12.5g Fat; 236 Calories

Shrimp In Curry Sauce

Servings: 2 | Cooking Time: 25 Minutes

Ingredients:
- ½ ounces grated Parmesan cheese
- 1 tbsp water
- 1 egg, beaten
- ¼ tsp curry powder
- 2 tsp almond flour
- 12 shrimp, shelled
- 3 tbsp coconut oil
- Sauce
- 2 tbsp curry leaves
- 2 tbsp butter
- ½ onion, diced
- ½ cup heavy cream
- ½ ounce cheddar

Directions:

1. Combine all dry ingredients for the batter. Melt the coconut oil in a skillet over medium heat. Dip the shrimp in the egg first, and then coat with the dry mixture. Fry until golden and crispy.
2. In another skillet, melt the butter. Add onion and cook for 3 minutes. Add curry leaves and cook for 30 seconds. Stir in heavy cream and cheddar and cook until thickened. Add the shrimp and coat well. Serve warm.

Nutrition Info:
- Per Servings 4.3g Carbs, 24.4g Protein, 41g Fat, 560 Calories

Tilapia With Olives & Tomato Sauce

Servings: 4 | Cooking Time: 30 Minutes

Ingredients:
- 4 tilapia fillets
- 2 garlic cloves, minced
- 2 tsp oregano
- 14 ounces diced tomatoes
- 1 tbsp olive oil
- ½ red onion, chopped
- 2 tbsp parsley
- ¼ cup kalamata olives

Directions:

1. Heat the olive oil in a skillet over medium heat and cook the onion for about 3 minutes. Add garlic and oregano and cook for 30 seconds. Stir in tomatoes and bring the mixture to a boil. Reduce the heat and simmer for 5 minutes. Add olives and tilapia, and cook for about 8 minutes. Serve the tilapia with tomato sauce.

Nutrition Info:
- Per Servings 6g Carbs, 23g Protein, 15g Fat, 282 Calories

Sour Cream Salmon With Parmesan

Servings: 4 | Cooking Time: 25 Minutes

Ingredients:
- 1 cup sour cream
- ½ tbsp minced dill
- ½ lemon, zested and juiced
- Pink salt and black pepper to season
- 4 salmon steaks
- ½ cup grated Parmesan cheese

Directions:

1. Preheat oven to 400ºF and line a baking sheet with parchment paper; set aside. In a bowl, mix the sour cream, dill, lemon zest, juice, salt and pepper, and set aside.
2. Season the fish with salt and black pepper, drizzle lemon juice on both sides of the fish and arrange them in the baking sheet. Spread the sour cream mixture on each fish and sprinkle with Parmesan.
3. Bake the fish for 15 minutes and after broil the top for 2 minutes with a close watch for a nice a brown color. Plate the fish and serve with buttery green beans.

Nutrition Info:
- Per Servings 1.2g Carbs, 16.2g Protein, 23.4g Fat, 288 Calories

Pistachio-crusted Salmon

Servings: 4 | Cooking Time: 35 Minutes

Ingredients:
- 4 salmon fillets
- ½ tsp pepper
- 1 tsp salt
- ¼ cup mayonnaise
- ½ cup chopped pistachios
- Sauce
- 1 chopped shallot
- 2 tsp lemon zest
- 1 tbsp olive oil
- A pinch of pepper
- 1 cup heavy cream

Directions:
1. Preheat the oven to 370ºF.
2. Brush the salmon with mayonnaise and season with salt and pepper. Coat with pistachios, place in a lined baking dish and bake for 15 minutes.
3. Heat the olive oil in a saucepan and sauté the shallot for 3 minutes. Stir in the rest of the sauce ingredients. Bring the mixture to a boil and cook until thickened. Serve the fish with the sauce.

Nutrition Info:
- Per Servings 6g Carbs, 34g Protein, 47g Fat, 563 Calories

Rosemary-lemon Shrimps

Servings: 4 | Cooking Time: 8 Minutes

Ingredients:
- 5 tablespoons butter
- ½ cup lemon juice, freshly squeezed
- 1 ½ lb. shrimps, peeled and deveined
- ¼ cup coconut aminos
- 1 tsp rosemary
- Pepper to taste

Directions:
1. Place all ingredients in a large pan on a high fire.
2. Boil for 8 minutes or until shrimps are pink.
3. Serve and enjoy.

Nutrition Info:
- Per Servings 3.7g Carbs, 35.8g Protein, 17.9g Fat, 315 Calories

Shrimp Spread

Servings: 20 | Cooking Time: 0 Minutes

Ingredients:
- 1 package cream cheese, softened
- 1/2 cup sour cream
- 1 cup seafood cocktail sauce
- 12 ounces frozen cooked salad shrimp, thawed
- 1 medium green pepper, chopped
- Pepper

Directions:
1. In a large bowl, beat the cream cheese, and sour cream until smooth.
2. Spread mixture on a round 12-inch serving platter.
3. Top with seafood sauce.
4. Sprinkle with shrimp and green peppers. Cover and refrigerate.
5. Serve with crackers.

Nutrition Info:
- Per Servings 4g Carbs, 8g Protein, 10g Fat, 136 Calories

Spicy Sea Bass With Hazelnuts

Servings: 2 | Cooking Time: 30 Minutes

Ingredients:
- 2 sea bass fillets
- 2 tbsp butter
- ⅓ cup roasted hazelnuts
- A pinch of cayenne pepper

Directions:
1. Preheat your oven to 425 °F. Line a baking dish with waxed paper. Melt the butter and brush it over the fish. In a food processor, combine the rest of the ingredients. Coat the sea bass with the hazelnut mixture. Place in the oven and bake for about 15 minutes.

Nutrition Info:
- Per Servings 2.8g Carbs, 40g Protein, 31g Fat, 467 Calories

Trout And Fennel Parcels

Servings: 4 | Cooking Time: 20 Minutes

Ingredients:
- ½ lb deboned trout, butterflied
- Salt and black pepper to season
- 3 tbsp olive oil + extra for tossing
- 4 sprigs rosemary
- 4 sprigs thyme
- 4 butter cubes
- 1 cup thinly sliced fennel
- 1 medium red onion, sliced
- 8 lemon slices
- 3 tsp capers to garnish

Directions:
1. Preheat the oven to 400ºF. Cut out parchment paper wide enough for each trout. In a bowl, toss the fennel and onion with a little bit of olive oil and share into the middle parts of the papers.
2. Place the fish on each veggie mound, top with a drizzle of olive oil each, salt and pepper, a sprig of rosemary and thyme, and 1 cube of butter. Also, lay the lemon slices on the fish. Wrap and close the fish packets securely, and place them on a baking sheet.
3. Bake in the oven for 15 minutes, and remove once ready. Plate them and garnish the fish with capers and serve with a squash mash.

Nutrition Info:
- Per Servings 2.8g Carbs, 17g Protein, 9.3g Fat, 234 Calories

Salmon Panzanella

Servings: 4 | Cooking Time: 22 Minutes

Ingredients:
- 1 lb skinned salmon, cut into 4 steaks each
- 1 cucumber, peeled, seeded, cubed
- Salt and black pepper to taste
- 8 black olives, pitted and chopped
- 1 tbsp capers, rinsed
- 2 large tomatoes, diced
- 3 tbsp red wine vinegar
- ¼ cup thinly sliced red onion
- 3 tbsp olive oil
- 2 slices day-old zero carb bread, cubed
- ¼ cup thinly sliced basil leaves

Directions:
1. Preheat a grill to 350ºF and prepare the salad. In a bowl, mix the cucumbers, olives, pepper, capers, tomatoes, wine vinegar, onion, olive oil, bread, and basil leaves. Let sit for the flavors to incorporate.
2. Season the salmon steaks with salt and pepper; grill them on both sides for 8 minutes in total. Serve the salmon steaks warm on a bed of the veggies' salad.

Nutrition Info:
- Per Servings 3.1g Carbs, 28.5g Protein, 21.7g Fat, 338 Calories

Chapter 5: Vegan, Vegetable & Meat-less Recipes

Roasted Leeks And Asparagus

Servings: 12 | Cooking Time: 25 Minutes

Ingredients:
- 3 pounds fresh asparagus, trimmed
- 2 medium leeks (white portion only), halved lengthwise
- 1-1/2 teaspoons dill weed
- 1/2 teaspoon crushed red pepper flakes
- 3 tablespoons melted butter
- 1/4 teaspoon pepper
- 1/2 teaspoon salt
- 4 ½ tablespoons olive oil

Directions:
1. Place asparagus and leeks on an ungreased 15x10x1-inch baking pan. Combine the remaining ingredients; pour over vegetables.
2. Bake at 400F for 20-25 minutes or until tender, stirring occasionally.

Nutrition Info:
- Per Servings 6g Carbs, 3g Protein, 8g Fat, 98 Calories

Sautéed Celeriac With Tomato Sauce

Servings: 4 | Cooking Time: 20 Minutes

Ingredients:
- 2 tbsp olive oil
- 1 garlic clove, crushed
- 1 celeriac, sliced
- ¼ cup vegetable stock
- Sea salt and black pepper, to taste
- For the Sauce
- 2 tomatoes, halved
- 2 tbsp olive oil
- ½ cup onions, chopped
- 2 cloves garlic, minced
- 1 chili, minced
- 1 bunch fresh basil, chopped
- 1 tbsp fresh cilantro, chopped
- Salt and black pepper, to taste

Directions:
1. Set a pan over medium-high heat and warm olive oil. Add in garlic and sauté for 1 minute. Stir in celeriac slices, stock and cook until softened. Sprinkle with black pepper and salt; kill the heat. Brush olive oil to the tomato halves. Microwave for 15 minutes; get rid of any excess liquid.
2. Remove the cooked tomatoes to a food processor; add the rest of the ingredients for the sauce and puree to obtain the desired consistency. Serve the celeriac topped with tomato sauce.

Nutrition Info:
- Per Servings 3g Carbs, 0.9g Protein, 13.6g Fat, 135 Calories

Avocado And Tomato Burritos

Servings: 4 | Cooking Time: 5 Minutes

Ingredients:
- 2 cups cauli rice
- Water for sprinkling
- 6 zero carb flatbread
- 2 cups sour cream sauce
- 1 ½ cups tomato herb salsa
- 2 avocados, peeled, pitted, sliced

Directions:
1. Pour the cauli rice in a bowl, sprinkle with water, and soften in the microwave for 2 minutes.
2. On flatbread, spread the sour cream all over and distribute the salsa on top. Top with cauli rice and scatter the avocado evenly on top. Fold and tuck the burritos and cut into two.

Nutrition Info:
- Per Servings 6g Carbs, 8g Protein, 25g Fat, 303 Calories

Vegan Cheesy Chips With Tomatoes

Servings: 6 | Cooking Time: 15 Minutes

Ingredients:
- 5 tomatoes, sliced
- ¼ cup olive oil
- 1 tbsp seasoning mix
- For Vegan cheese
- ½ cup pepitas seeds
- 1 tbsp nutritional yeast
- Salt and black pepper, to taste
- 1 tsp garlic puree

Directions:
1. Over the sliced tomatoes, drizzle olive oil. Set oven to 200ºF.
2. In a food processor, add all vegan cheese ingredients and pulse until the desired consistency is attained. Combine vegan cheese and seasoning mixture. Toss in seasoned tomato slices to coat.
3. Set the tomato slices on the prepared baking pan and bake for 10 minutes.

Nutrition Info:
- Per Servings 7.2g Carbs, 4.6g Protein, 14g Fat, 161 Calories

Cilantro-lime Guacamole

Servings: 4 | Cooking Time: 10 Minutes

Ingredients:
- 3 avocados, peeled, pitted, and mashed
- 1 lime, juiced
- 1/2 cup diced onion
- 3 tablespoons chopped fresh cilantro
- 2 Roma (plum) tomatoes, diced
- 1 teaspoon salt
- 1 teaspoon minced garlic
- 1 pinch ground cayenne pepper (optional)
- 1 teaspoon minced garlic

Directions:
1. In a mixing bowl, mash the avocados with a fork. Sprinkle with salt and lime juice.
2. Stir together diced onion, tomatoes, cilantro, pepper and garlic.
3. Serve immediately, or refrigerate until ready to serve.

Nutrition Info:
- Per Servings 8g Carbs, 19g Protein, 22.2g Fat, 362 Calories

Spiced Cauliflower & Peppers

Servings: 4 | Cooking Time: 35 Minutes

Ingredients:
- 1 pound cauliflower, cut into florets
- 2 bell peppers, halved
- ¼ cup olive oil
- Sea salt and black pepper, to taste
- ½ tsp cayenne pepper
- 1 tsp curry powder

Directions:
1. Set oven to 425 °F. Line a parchment paper to a large baking sheet. Sprinkle olive oil to the peppers and cauliflower alongside curry powder, black pepper, salt, and cayenne pepper.
2. Set the vegetables on the baking sheet. Roast for 30 minutes as you toss in intervals until they start to brown. Serve alongside mushroom pate or homemade tomato dip!

Nutrition Info:
- Per Servings 7.4g Carbs, 3g Protein, 13.9g Fat, 166 Calories

Cauliflower Risotto With Mushrooms

Servings: 4 | Cooking Time: 15 Minutes

Ingredients:
- 2 shallots, diced
- 3 tbsp olive oil
- ¼ cup veggie broth
- ⅓ cup Parmesan cheese
- 4 tbsp butter
- 3 tbsp chopped chives
- 2 pounds mushrooms, sliced
- 4 ½ cups riced cauliflower

Directions:
1. Heat 2 tbsp. oil in a saucepan. Add the mushrooms and cook over medium heat for about 3 minutes. Remove from the pan and set aside.
2. Heat the remaining oil and cook the shallots for 2 minutes. Stir in the cauliflower and broth, and cook until the liquid is absorbed. Stir in the rest of the ingredients.

Nutrition Info:
- Per Servings 8.4g Carbs, 11g Protein, 18g Fat, 264 Calories

Stuffed Portobello Mushrooms

Servings: 2 | Cooking Time: 30 Minutes

Ingredients:
- 4 portobello mushrooms, stems removed
- 2 tbsp olive oil
- 2 cups lettuce
- 1 cup crumbled blue cheese

Directions:
1. Preheat the oven to 350ºF. Fill the mushrooms with blue cheese and place on a lined baking sheet; bake for 20 minutes. Serve with lettuce drizzled with olive oil.

Nutrition Info:
- Per Servings 5.5g Carbs, 14g Protein, 29g Fat, 334 Calories

Paprika 'n Cajun Seasoned Onion Rings

Servings: 6 | Cooking Time: 25 Minutes

Ingredients:
- 1 large white onion
- 2 large eggs, beaten
- ½ teaspoon Cajun seasoning
- ¾ cup almond flour
- 1 ½ teaspoon paprika
- ½ cups coconut oil for frying
- ¼ cup water
- Salt and pepper to taste

Directions:
1. Preheat a pot with oil for 8 minutes.
2. Peel the onion, cut off the top and slice into circles.
3. In a mixing bowl, combine the water and the eggs. Season with pepper and salt.
4. Soak the onion in the egg mixture.
5. In another bowl, combine the almond flour, paprika powder, Cajun seasoning, salt and pepper.
6. Dredge the onion in the almond flour mixture.
7. Place in the pot and cook in batches until golden brown, around 8 minutes per batch.

Nutrition Info:
- Per Servings 3.9g Carbs, 2.8g Protein, 24.1g Fat, 262 Calories

Guacamole

Servings: 2 | Cooking Time: 0 Minutes

Ingredients:
- 2 medium ripe avocados
- 1 tablespoon lemon juice
- 1/4 cup chopped tomatoes
- 4 tablespoons olive oil
- 1/4 teaspoon salt
- Pepper to taste

Directions:
1. Peel and chop avocados; place them in a small bowl. Sprinkle with lemon juice.
2. Add tomatoes and salt.
3. Season with pepper to taste and mash coarsely with a fork. Refrigerate until serving.

Nutrition Info:
- Per Servings 10g Carbs, 6g Protein, 56g Fat, 565 Calories

Tasty Cauliflower Dip

Servings: 4 | Cooking Time: 10 Minutes

Ingredients:
- ¾ pound cauliflower, cut into florets
- ¼ cup olive oil
- Salt and black pepper, to taste
- 1 garlic clove, smashed
- 1 tbsp sesame paste
- 1 tbsp fresh lime juice
- ½ tsp garam masala

Directions:
1. Steam cauliflower until tender for 7 minutes in. Transfer to a blender and pulse until you attain a rice-like consistency.
2. Place in Garam Masala, oil, black paper, fresh lime juice, garlic, salt, and sesame paste. Blend the mixture until well combined. Decorate with some additional olive oil and serve. Otherwise, refrigerate until ready to use.

Nutrition Info:
- Per Servings 4.7g Carbs, 3.7g Protein, 8.2g Fat, 100 Calories

Classic Tangy Ratatouille

Servings: 6 | Cooking Time: 47 Minutes

Ingredients:
- 2 eggplants, chopped
- 3 zucchinis, chopped
- 2 red onions, diced
- 1 can tomatoes
- 2 red bell peppers, cut in chunks
- 1 yellow bell pepper, cut in chunks
- 3 cloves garlic, sliced
- ½ cup basil leaves, chop half
- 4 sprigs thyme
- 1 tbsp balsamic vinegar
- 2 tbsp olive oil
- ½ lemon, zested

Directions:
1. In a casserole pot, heat the olive oil and sauté the eggplants, zucchinis, and bell peppers over medium heat for 5 minutes. Spoon the veggies into a large bowl.
2. In the same pan, sauté garlic, onions, and thyme leaves for 5 minutes and return the cooked veggies to the pan along with the canned tomatoes, balsamic vinegar, chopped basil, salt, and pepper to taste. Stir and cover the pot, and cook the ingredients on low heat for 30 minutes.
3. Open the lid and stir in the remaining basil leaves, lemon zest, and adjust the seasoning. Turn the heat off. Plate the ratatouille and serve with some low carb crusted bread.

Nutrition Info:
- Per Servings 5.6g Carbs, 1.7g Protein, 12.1g Fat, 154 Calories

Zucchini Garlic Fries

Servings: 6 | Cooking Time: 25 Minutes

Ingredients:
- ¼ teaspoon garlic powder
- ½ cup almond flour
- 2 large egg, beaten
- 3 medium zucchinis, sliced into fry sticks
- 3 tablespoons olive oil
- Salt and pepper to taste

Directions:
1. Preheat oven to 400oF.
2. Mix all ingredients in a bowl until the zucchini fries are well coated.
3. Place fries on a cookie sheet and spread evenly.
4. Put in the oven and cook for 15 minutes.
5. Stir fries, continue baking for an additional 10 minutes.

Nutrition Info:
- Per Servings 0.5g Carbs, 2g Protein, 8g Fat, 80 Calories

Bell Pepper & Pumpkin With Avocado Sauce

Servings: 4 | Cooking Time: 15 Minutes

Ingredients:
- ½ pound pumpkin, peeled
- ½ pound bell peppers
- 1 tbsp olive oil
- 1 avocado, peeled and pitted
- 1 lemon, juiced and zested
- 2 tbsp sesame oil
- 2 tbsp cilantro, chopped
- 1 onion, chopped
- 1 jalapeño pepper, deveined and minced
- Salt and black pepper, to taste

Directions:
1. Use a spiralizer to spiralize bell peppers and pumpkin. Using a large nonstick skillet, warm olive oil. Add in bell peppers and pumpkin and sauté for 8 minutes.
2. Combine the remaining ingredients to obtain a creamy mixture. Top the vegetable noodles with the avocado sauce and serve.

Nutrition Info:
- Per Servings 11g Carbs, 1.9g Protein, 20.2g Fat, 233 Calories

Fried Tofu With Mushrooms

Servings: 2 | Cooking Time: 40 Minutes

Ingredients:
- 12 ounces extra firm tofu, pressed and cubed
- 1 ½ tbsp flax seed meal
- Salt and black pepper, to taste
- 1 tsp garlic clove, minced
- ½ tsp paprika
- 1 tsp onion powder
- ½ tsp ground bay leaf
- 1 tbsp olive oil
- 1 cup mushrooms, sliced
- 1 jalapeño pepper, deveined, sliced

Directions:
1. In a container, add onion powder, tofu, salt, paprika, black pepper, flaxseed, garlic paste, and bay leaf. While the container is closed, toss the mixture to coat, and allow to marinate for 30 minutes.
2. In a pan, warm oil over medium heat. Cook mushrooms and tofu for 6 minutes, stirring continuously.

Nutrition Info:
- Per Servings 8.1g Carbs, 15.6g Protein, 15.9g Fat, 223 Calories

Roasted Asparagus With Spicy Eggplant Dip

Servings: 6 | Cooking Time: 35 Minutes

Ingredients:
- 1 ½ pounds asparagus spears, trimmed
- ¼ cup olive oil
- 1 tsp sea salt
- ½ tsp black pepper, to taste
- ½ tsp paprika
- For Eggplant Dip
- ¾ pound eggplants
- 2 tsp olive oil
- ½ cup scallions, chopped
- 2 cloves garlic, minced
- 1 tbsp fresh lemon juice
- ½ tsp chili pepper
- Salt and black pepper, to taste
- ¼ cup fresh cilantro, chopped

Directions:
1. Set the oven to 390ºF. Line a parchment paper to a baking sheet. Add asparagus spears to the baking sheet. Toss with oil, paprika, pepper, and salt. Bake until cooked through for 9 minutes.
2. Set the oven to 425 ºF. Add eggplants on a lined cookie sheet. Place under the broiler for about 20 minutes; let the eggplants to cool. Peel them and discard the stems. Place a frying pan over medium-high heat and warm olive oil. Add in garlic and onion and sauté until tender.
3. Using a food processor, pulse together black pepper, roasted eggplants, salt, lemon juice, scallion mixture, and chili pepper to mix evenly. Add cilantro for garnishing. Serve alongside roasted asparagus spears.

Nutrition Info:
- Per Servings 9g Carbs, 3.6g Protein, 12.1g Fat, 149 Calories

Cream Of Zucchini And Avocado

Servings: 4 | Cooking Time: 35 Minutes

Ingredients:
- 3 tsp vegetable oil
- 1 onion, chopped
- 1 carrot, sliced
- 1 turnip, sliced
- 3 cups zucchinis, chopped
- 1 avocado, peeled and diced
- ¼ tsp ground black pepper
- 4 vegetable broth
- 1 tomato, pureed

Directions:

1. In a pot, warm the oil and sauté onion until translucent, about 3 minutes. Add in turnip, zucchini, and carrot and cook for 7 minutes; add black pepper for seasoning.
2. Mix in pureed tomato, and broth; and boil. Change heat to low and allow the mixture to simmer for 20 minutes. Lift from the heat. In batches, add the soup and avocado to a blender. Blend until creamy and smooth.

Nutrition Info:
- Per Servings 11g Carbs, 2.2g Protein, 13.4g Fat, 165 Calories

Keto Cauliflower Hash Browns

Servings: 4 | Cooking Time: 30 Mins

Ingredients:
- 1 lb cauliflower
- 3 eggs
- ½ yellow onion, grated
- 2 pinches pepper
- 4 oz. butter, for frying
- What you'll need from the store cupboard:
- 1 tsp salt

Directions:

1. Rinse, trim and grate the cauliflower using a food processor or grater.
2. In a large bowl, add the cauliflower onion and pepper, tossing evenly. Set aside for 5 to 10 minutes.
3. In a large skillet over medium heat, heat a generous amount of butter on medium heat. The cooking process will go quicker if you plan to have room for 3–4 pancakes at a time. Use the oven on low heat to keep the first batches of pancakes warm while you make the others.
4. Place scoops of the grated cauliflower mixture in the frying pan and flatten them carefully until they measure about 3 to 4 inches in diameter.
5. Fry for 4 to 5 minutes on each side. Adjust the heat to make sure they don't burn. Serve.

Nutrition Info:
- Per Servings 5g Carbs, 7g Protein, 26g Fat, 282 Calories

Cauliflower Fritters

Servings: 6 | Cooking Time: 15 Minutes

Ingredients:
- 1 large cauliflower head, cut into florets
- 2 eggs, beaten
- ½ teaspoon turmeric
- 1 large onion, peeled and chopped
- ½ teaspoon salt
- ¼ teaspoon black pepper
- 6 tablespoons oil

Directions:
1. Place the cauliflower florets in a pot with water.
2. Bring to a boil and drain once cooked.
3. Place the cauliflower, eggs, onion, turmeric, salt, and pepper into the food processor.
4. Pulse until the mixture becomes coarse.
5. Transfer into a bowl. Using your hands, form six small flattened balls and place in the fridge for at least 1 hour until the mixture hardens.
6. Heat the oil in a skillet and fry the cauliflower patties for 3 minutes on each side.
7. Serve and enjoy.

Nutrition Info:
- Per Servings 2.28g Carbs, 3.9g Protein, 15.3g Fat, 157 Calories

Curried Tofu

Servings: 6 | Cooking Time: 15 Minutes

Ingredients:
- 2 cloves of garlic, minced
- 1 onion, cubed
- 12-ounce firm tofu, drained and cubed
- 1 teaspoon curry powder
- 1 tablespoon soy sauce
- ¼ teaspoon pepper
- 5 tablespoons olive oil

Directions:
1. Heat the oil in a skillet over medium flame.
2. Sauté the garlic and onion until fragrant.
3. Stir in the tofu and stir for 3 minutes.
4. Add the rest of the ingredients and adjust the water.
5. Close the lid and allow simmering for 10 minutes.
6. Serve and enjoy.

Nutrition Info:
- Per Servings 4.4g Carbs, 6.2g Protein, 14.1g Fat, 148 Calories

Easy Cauliflower Soup

Servings: 4 | Cooking Time: 15 Minutes

Ingredients:
- 2 tbsp olive oil
- 2 onions, finely chopped
- 1 tsp garlic, minced
- 1 pound cauliflower, cut into florets
- 1 cup kale, chopped
- 4 cups vegetable broth
- ½ cup almond milk
- ½ tsp salt
- ½ tsp red pepper flakes
- 1 tbsp fresh chopped parsley

Directions:
1. Set a pot over medium-high heat and warm the oil. Add garlic and onion and sauté until browned and softened. Place in vegetable broth, kale, and cauliflower; cook for 10 minutes until the mixture boils. Stir in the pepper, salt, and almond milk; simmer the soup while covered for 5 minutes.
2. Transfer the soup to an immersion blender and blend to achieve the required consistency; top with parsley and serve immediately.

Nutrition Info:
- Per Servings 11.8g Carbs, 8.1g Protein, 10.3g Fat, 172 Calories

Crispy-topped Baked Vegetables

Servings: 4 | Cooking Time: 40 Minutes

Ingredients:
- 2 tbsp olive oil
- 1 onion, chopped
- 1 celery, chopped
- 2 carrots, grated
- ½ pound turnip, sliced
- 1 cup vegetable broth
- 1 tsp turmeric
- Sea salt and black pepper, to taste
- ½ tsp liquid smoke
- 1 cup Parmesan cheese, shredded
- 2 tbsp fresh chives, chopped

Directions:
1. Set oven to 360ºF. Grease a baking dish with olive oil. Set a skillet over medium-high heat and warm olive oil. Sweat the onion until soft. Place in the turnip slices and celery. Cook for 4 minutes.
2. Remove the vegetable mixture to the baking dish. Combine vegetable broth with turmeric, black pepper, liquid smoke, and salt.
3. Spread this mixture over the vegetables. Apply a topping of vegan parmesan cheese and bake for about 30 minutes. Decorate with fresh chives and serve.

Nutrition Info:
- Per Servings 8.6g Carbs, 16.3g Protein, 16.3g Fat, 242 Calories

Greek-style Zucchini Pasta

Servings: 4 | Cooking Time: 15 Minutes

Ingredients:
- ¼ cup sun-dried tomatoes
- 5 garlic cloves, minced
- 2 tbsp butter
- 1 cup spinach
- 2 large zucchinis, spiralized
- ¼ cup crumbled feta
- ¼ cup Parmesan cheese, shredded
- 10 kalamata olives, halved
- 2 tbsp olive oil
- 2 tbsp chopped parsley

Directions:
1. Heat the olive oil in a pan over medium heat. Add zoodles, butter, garlic, and spinach. Cook for about 5 minutes. Stir in the olives, tomatoes, and parsley. Cook for 2 more minutes. Add in the cheeses and serve.

Nutrition Info:
- Per Servings 6.5g Carbs, 6.5g Protein, 19.5g Fat, 231 Calories

Greek Salad With Poppy Seed Dressing

Servings: 4 | Cooking Time: 3 Hours 15 Minutes

Ingredients:
- For the Dressing
- 1 cup poppy seeds
- 2 cups water
- 2 tbsp green onions, chopped
- 1 garlic clove, minced
- 1 lime, freshly squeezed
- Salt and black pepper, to taste
- ¼ tsp dill, minced
- 2 tbsp almond milk
- For the salad
- 1 head lettuce, separated into leaves
- 3 tomatoes, diced
- 3 cucumbers, sliced
- 2 tbsp kalamata olives, pitted

Directions:
1. Put all dressing ingredients in a food processor and pulse until well incorporated. Add in poppy seeds and mix well. Divide salad ingredients into 4 plates. Add the dressing to each and shake.

Nutrition Info:
- Per Servings 6.7g Carbs, 7.6g Protein, 15.6g Fat, 208 Calories

Cauliflower Gouda Casserole

Servings: 4 | Cooking Time: 21 Minutes

Ingredients:
- 2 heads cauliflower, cut into florets
- ⅓ cup butter, cubed
- 2 tbsp melted butter
- 1 white onion, chopped
- Pink salt and black pepper to taste
- ¼ almond milk
- ½ cup almond flour
- 1 ½ cup grated gouda cheese
- Water for sprinkling

Directions:
1. Preheat oven to 350ºF and put the cauli florets in a large microwave-safe bowl. Sprinkle with water, and steam in the microwave for 4 to 5 minutes.
2. Melt the ⅓ cup of butter in a saucepan over medium heat and sauté the onion for 3 minutes. Add the cauliflower, season with salt and black pepper and mix in almond milk. Simmer for 3 minutes.
3. Mix the remaining melted butter with almond flour. Stir into the cauliflower as well as half of the cheese. Sprinkle the top with the remaining cheese and bake for 10 minutes until the cheese has melted and golden brown on the top. Plate the bake and serve with arugula salad.

Nutrition Info:
- Per Servings 4g Carbs, 12g Protein, 15g Fat, 215 Calories

Chapter 6: Soups, Stew & Salads Recipes

Cream Of Thyme Tomato Soup

Servings: 6 | Cooking Time: 20 Minutes

Ingredients:
- 2 tbsp ghee
- 2 large red onions, diced
- ½ cup raw cashew nuts, diced
- 2 cans tomatoes
- 1 tsp fresh thyme leaves + extra to garnish
- 1 ½ cups water
- Salt and black pepper to taste
- 1 cup heavy cream

Directions:
1. Melt ghee in a pot over medium heat and sauté the onions for 4 minutes until softened.
2. Stir in the tomatoes, thyme, water, cashews, and season with salt and black pepper. Cover and bring to simmer for 10 minutes until thoroughly cooked.
3. Open, turn the heat off, and puree the ingredients with an immersion blender. Adjust to taste and stir in the heavy cream. Spoon into soup bowls and serve with low carb parmesan cheese toasts.

Nutrition Info:
- Per Servings 3g Carbs, 11g Protein, 27g Fat, 310 Calories

Simplified French Onion Soup

Servings: 5 | Cooking Time: 30 Minutes

Ingredients:
- 3 large onions, sliced
- 2 bay leaves
- 5 cups Beef Bone Broth
- 1 teaspoon dried thyme
- 1-oz Gruyere cheese, sliced into 5 equal pieces
- Pepper to taste
- 4 tablespoons oil

Directions:
1. Place a heavy-bottomed pot on medium-high fire and heat pot for 3 minutes.
2. Add oil and heat for 2 minutes. Stir in onions and sauté for 5 minutes.
3. Lower fire to medium-low, continue sautéing onions for 10 minutes until soft and browned, but not burned.
4. Add remaining ingredients and mix well.
5. Bring to a boil, lower fire to a simmer, cover and cook for 5 minutes.
6. Ladle into bowls, top with cheese.
7. Let it sit for 5 minutes.
8. Serve and enjoy.

Nutrition Info:
- Per Servings 9.9g Carbs, 4.3g Protein, 16.8g Fat, 208 Calories

Warm Baby Artichoke Salad

Servings: 4 | Cooking Time: 30 Minutes

Ingredients:
- 6 baby artichokes
- 6 cups water
- 1 tbsp lemon juice
- ¼ cup cherry peppers, halved
- ¼ cup pitted olives, sliced
- ¼ cup olive oil
- ¼ tsp lemon zest
- 2 tsp balsamic vinegar, sugar-free
- 1 tbsp chopped dill
- ½ tsp salt
- ¼ tsp black pepper
- 1 tbsp capers
- ¼ tsp caper brine

Directions:

1. Combine the water and salt in a pot over medium heat. Trim and halve the artichokes; add to the pot. Bring to a boil, lower the heat, and let simmer for 20 minutes until tender.
2. Combine the rest of the ingredients, except the olives in a bowl. Drain and place the artichokes in a serving plate. Pour the prepared mixture over; toss to combine well. Serve topped with the olives.

Nutrition Info:
- Per Servings 5g Carbs, 1g Protein, 13g Fat, 170 Calories

Power Green Soup

Servings: 6 | Cooking Time: 30 Minutes

Ingredients:
- 1 broccoli head, chopped
- 1 cup spinach
- 1 onion, chopped
- 2 garlic cloves, minced
- ½ cup watercress
- 5 cups veggie stock
- 1 cup coconut milk
- 1 tsp salt
- 1 tbsp ghee
- 1 bay leaf
- Salt and black pepper, to taste

Directions:

1. Melt the ghee in a large pot over medium heat. Add onion and cook for 3 minutes. Add garlic and cook for another minute. Add broccoli and cook for an additional 5 minutes.
2. Pour the stock over and add the bay leaf. Close the lid, bring to a boil, and reduce the heat. Simmer for about 3 minutes.
3. In the end, add spinach and watercress, and cook for 3 more minutes. Stir in the coconut cream, salt and pepper. Discard the bay leaf, and blend the soup with a hand blender.

Nutrition Info:
- Per Servings 5.8g Carbs, 4.9g Protein, 37.6g Fat, 392 Calories

Caesar Salad With Chicken And Parmesan

Servings: 4 | Cooking Time: 1 Hour And 30 Minutes

Ingredients:
- 4 boneless, skinless chicken thighs
- ¼ cup lemon juice
- 2 garlic cloves, minced
- 4 tbsp olive oil
- ½ cup caesar salad dressing, sugar-free
- 12 bok choy leaves
- 3 Parmesan crisps
- Parmesan cheese, grated for garnishing

Directions:

1. Combine the chicken, lemon juice, 2 tbsp of olive oil, and garlic in a Ziploc bag. Seal the bag, shake to combine, and refrigerate for 1 hour. Preheat the grill to medium heat and grill the chicken for about 4 minutes per side.

2. Cut the bok choy leaves lengthwise, and brush it with the remaining olive oil. Grill the bok choy for about 3 minutes. Place on a serving bowl. Top with the chicken and drizzle the caesar salad dressing over. Top with parmesan crisps and sprinkle the grated parmesan cheese over.

Nutrition Info:
- Per Servings 5g Carbs, 33g Protein, 39g Fat, 529 Calories

Garlic Chicken Salad

Servings: 4 | Cooking Time: 15 Minutes

Ingredients:
- 2 chicken breasts, boneless, skinless, flattened
- Salt and black pepper to taste
- 2 tbsp garlic powder
- 1 tsp olive oil
- 1 ½ cups mixed salad greens
- 1 tbsp red wine vinegar
- 1 cup crumbled blue cheese

Directions:

1. Season the chicken with salt, black pepper, and garlic powder. Heat oil in a pan over high heat and fry the chicken for 4 minutes on both sides until golden brown. Remove chicken to a cutting board and let cool before slicing.

2. Toss salad greens with red wine vinegar and share the salads into 4 plates. Divide chicken slices on top and sprinkle with blue cheese. Serve salad with carrots fries.

Nutrition Info:
- Per Servings 4g Carbs, 14g Protein, 23g Fat, 286 Calories

Creamy Cauliflower Soup With Chorizo Sausage

Servings: 4 | Cooking Time: 40 Minutes

Ingredients:
- 1 cauliflower head, chopped
- 1 turnip, chopped
- 3 tbsp butter
- 1 chorizo sausage, sliced
- 2 cups chicken broth
- 1 small onion, chopped
- 2 cups water
- Salt and black pepper, to taste

Directions:

1. Melt 2 tbsp. of the butter in a large pot over medium heat. Stir in onion and cook until soft and golden, about 3-4 minutes. Add cauliflower and turnip, and cook for another 5 minutes.
2. Pour the broth and water over. Bring to a boil, simmer covered, and cook for about 20 minutes until the vegetables are tender. Remove from heat. Melt the remaining butter in a skillet. Add the chorizo sausage and cook for 5 minutes until crispy. Puree the soup with a hand blender until smooth. Taste and adjust the seasonings. Serve the soup in deep bowls topped with the chorizo sausage.

Nutrition Info:
- Per Servings 5.7g Carbs, 10g Protein, 19.1g Fat, 251 Calories

Pork Burger Salad With Yellow Cheddar

Servings: 4 | Cooking Time: 25 Minutes

Ingredients:
- 1 lb ground pork
- Salt and black pepper to season
- 1 tbsp olive oil
- 2 hearts romaine lettuce, torn into pieces
- 2 firm tomatoes, sliced
- ¼ red onion, sliced
- 3 oz yellow cheddar cheese, shredded

Directions:

1. Season the pork with salt and black pepper, mix and make medium-sized patties out of them.
2. Heat the oil in a skillet over medium heat and fry the patties on both sides for 10 minutes until browned and cook within. Transfer to a wire rack to drain oil. When cooled, cut into quarters.
3. Mix the lettuce, tomatoes, and red onion in a salad bowl, season with a little oil, salt, and pepper. Toss and add the pork on top.
4. Melt the cheese in the microwave for about 90 seconds. Drizzle the cheese over the salad and serve.

Nutrition Info:
- Per Servings 2g Carbs, 22g Protein, 23g Fat, 310 Calories

Green Salad With Bacon And Blue Cheese

Servings: 4 | Cooking Time: 15 Minutes

Ingredients:
- 2 pack mixed salad greens
- 8 strips bacon
- 1 ½ cups crumbled blue cheese
- 1 tbsp white wine vinegar
- 3 tbsp extra virgin olive oil
- Salt and black pepper to taste

Directions:

1. Pour the salad greens in a salad bowl; set aside. Fry bacon strips in a skillet over medium heat for 6 minutes, until browned and crispy. Chop the bacon and scatter over the salad. Add in half of the cheese, toss and set aside.

2. In a small bowl, whisk the white wine vinegar, olive oil, salt, and black pepper until dressing is well combined. Drizzle half of the dressing over the salad, toss, and top with remaining cheese. Divide salad into four plates and serve with crusted chicken fries along with remaining dressing.

Nutrition Info:
- Per Servings 2g Carbs, 4g Protein, 20g Fat, 205 Calories

Creamy Cauliflower Soup With Bacon Chips

Servings: 4 | Cooking Time: 25 Minutes

Ingredients:
- 2 tbsp ghee
- 1 onion, chopped
- 2 head cauliflower, cut into florets
- 2 cups water
- Salt and black pepper to taste
- 3 cups almond milk
- 1 cup shredded white cheddar cheese
- 3 bacon strips

Directions:

1. Melt the ghee in a saucepan over medium heat and sauté the onion for 3 minutes until fragrant.

2. Include the cauli florets, sauté for 3 minutes to slightly soften, add the water, and season with salt and black pepper. Bring to a boil, and then reduce the heat to low. Cover and cook for 10 minutes.

3. Puree cauliflower with an immersion blender until the ingredients are evenly combined and stir in the almond milk and cheese until the cheese melts. Adjust taste with salt and black pepper.

4. In a non-stick skillet over high heat, fry the bacon, until crispy. Divide soup between serving bowls, top with crispy bacon, and serve hot.

Nutrition Info:
- Per Servings 6g Carbs, 8g Protein, 37g Fat, 402 Calories

Creamy Cauliflower Soup

Servings: 4 | Cooking Time: 20 Minutes

Ingredients:
- 1 cauliflower head, chopped
- ½ cup onions, chopped
- 4 cups chicken broth
- 1 tablespoon butter
- 1 cup heavy cream
- Pepper and salt to taste

Directions:
1. Place all ingredients in a pot on medium-high fire, except for the heavy cream.
2. Season with salt and pepper to taste.
3. Give a good stir to combine everything.
4. Cover and bring to a boil, and simmer for 15 minutes.
5. With an immersion blender, blend well until smooth and creamy.
6. Stir in heavy cream and continue simmering for another 5 minutes. Adjust seasoning if needed.
7. Serve and enjoy.

Nutrition Info:
- Per Servings 7.3g Carbs, 53.9g Protein, 30.8g Fat, 531 Calories

Strawberry, Mozzarella Salad

Servings: 3 | Cooking Time: 10 Minutes

Ingredients:
- 5 ounces organic salad greens of your choice
- 2 medium cucumber, spiralized
- 2 cups strawberries, hulled and chopped
- 8 ounces mini mozzarella cheese balls
- ½ cup balsamic vinegar
- 5 tablespoons olive oil
- Salt to taste

Directions:
1. Toss all ingredients in a salad bowl.
2. Allow chilling in the fridge for at least 10 minutes before serving.

Nutrition Info:
- Per Servings 10g Carbs, 7g Protein, 31g Fat, 351 Calories

Chicken Taco Soup

Servings: 6 | Cooking Time: 45 Minutes

Ingredients:
- 1-pound boneless chicken breast
- 1 tbsp taco seasoning
- 3 medium tomato chopped
- 1 medium onion chopped
- 2 Tablespoons garlic minced
- 5 cups water
- Salt and Pepper to taste
- Sour cream or tortilla chips for topping (optional)

Directions:
1. Add all ingredients in a heavy-bottomed pot except for garnish if using.
2. Bring to a boil, lower fire to a simmer, cover and cook for 30 minutes.
3. Remove chicken and shred. Return to the pot. Adjust seasoning with pepper and salt to taste.
4. Serve and enjoy with topping.

Nutrition Info:
- Per Servings 5.0g Carbs, 15.0g Protein, 2.0g Fat, 98 Calories

Pumpkin & Meat Peanut Stew

Servings: 6 | Cooking Time: 45 Minutes

Ingredients:
- 1 cup pumpkin puree
- 2 pounds chopped pork stew meat
- 1 tbsp peanut butter
- 4 tbsp chopped peanuts
- 1 garlic clove, minced
- ½ cup chopped onion
- ½ cup white wine
- 1 tbsp olive oil
- 1 tsp lemon juice
- ¼ cup granulated sweetener
- ¼ tsp cardamom
- ¼ tsp allspice
- 2 cups water
- 2 cups chicken stock

Directions:
1. Heat the olive oil in a large pot and sauté onion for 3 minutes, until translucent. Add garlic and cook for 30 more seconds. Add the pork and cook until browned, about 5-6 minutes, stirring occasionally. Pour in the wine and cook for one minute.
2. Add in the remaining ingredients, except for the lemon juice and peanuts. Bring the mixture to a boil, and cook for 5 minutes. Reduce the heat to low, cover the pot, and let cook for about 30 minutes. Adjust seasoning and stir in the lemon juice before serving.
3. Ladle into serving bowls and serve topped with peanuts.

Nutrition Info:
- Per Servings 4g Carbs, 27.5g Protein, 33g Fat, 451 Calories

Mushroom-broccoli Soup

Servings: 4 | Cooking Time: 20 Minutes

Ingredients:
- 1 onion, diced
- 3 cloves of garlic, diced
- 2 cups mushrooms, chopped
- 2 heads of broccoli, cut into florets
- 1 cup full-fat milk
- 3 cups water
- Pepper and salt to taste

Directions:
1. Place a heavy-bottomed pot on medium-high fire and heat for 3 minutes.
2. Add onion, garlic, water, and broccoli. Season generously with pepper and salt.
3. Cover and bring to a boil. Once boiling, lower fire to a simmer and let it cook for 7 minutes.
4. With a handheld blender, puree mixture until smooth and creamy.
5. Stir in mushrooms and milk, cover, and simmer for another 8 minutes.
6. Serve and enjoy.

Nutrition Info:
- Per Servings 8.5g Carbs, 3.8g Protein, 1.0g Fat, 58.2 Calories

Brazilian Moqueca (shrimp Stew)

Servings: 6 | Cooking Time: 25 Minutes

Ingredients:
- 1 cup coconut milk
- 2 tbsp lime juice
- ¼ cup diced roasted peppers
- 1 ½ pounds shrimp, peeled and deveined
- ¼ cup olive oil
- 1 garlic clove, minced
- 14 ounces diced tomatoes
- 2 tbsp sriracha sauce
- 1 chopped onion
- ¼ cup chopped cilantro
- Fresh dill, chopped to garnish
- Salt and black pepper, to taste

Directions:
1. Heat the olive oil in a pot over medium heat. Add onion and cook for 3 minutes or until translucent. Add the garlic and cook for another minute, until soft. Add tomatoes, shrimp, and cilantro. Cook until the shrimp becomes opaque, about 3-4 minutes.
2. Stir in sriracha sauce and coconut milk, and cook for 2 minutes. Do not bring to a boil. Stir in the lime juice and season with salt and pepper. Spoon the stew in bowls, garnish with fresh dill to serve.

Nutrition Info:
- Per Servings 5g Carbs, 23.1g Protein, 21g Fat, 324 Calories

Caesar Salad With Smoked Salmon And Poached Eggs

Servings: 4 | Cooking Time: 15 Minutes

Ingredients:
- 3 cups water
- 8 eggs
- 2 cups torn romaine lettuce
- ½ cup smoked salmon, chopped
- 6 slices bacon
- 2 tbsp Heinz low carb Caesar dressing

Directions:

1. Boil the water in a pot over medium heat for 5 minutes and bring to simmer. Crack each egg into a small bowl and gently slide into the water. Poach for 2 to 3 minutes, remove with a perforated spoon, transfer to a paper towel to dry, and plate. Poach the remaining 7 eggs.

2. Put the bacon in a skillet and fry over medium heat until browned and crispy, about 6 minutes, turning once. Remove, allow cooling, and chop in small pieces.

3. Toss the lettuce, smoked salmon, bacon, and caesar dressing in a salad bowl. Divide the salad into 4 plates, top with two eggs each, and serve immediately or chilled.

Nutrition Info:
- Per Servings 5g Carbs, 8g Protein, 21g Fat, 260 Calories

Creamy Soup With Greens

Servings: 6 | Cooking Time: 20 Minutes

Ingredients:
- ½-pounds collard greens, torn to bite-sized pieces
- 5 cups chicken broth
- 2 cups broccoli florets
- 1 cup diced onion
- 3 tablespoon oil
- 4 tablespoons butter
- Salt and pepper to taste

Directions:

1. Add all ingredients to the pot and bring to a boil.
2. Lower fire to a simmer and simmer for 15 minutes while covered.
3. With an immersion blender, puree soup until creamy.
4. Adjust seasoning to taste.
5. Serve and enjoy.

Nutrition Info:
- Per Servings 6.5g Carbs, 50.6g Protein, 33.5g Fat, 548 Calories

Broccoli Slaw Salad With Mustard-mayo Dressing

Servings: 6 | Cooking Time: 10 Minutes

Ingredients:
- 2 tbsp granulated swerve
- 1 tbsp Dijon mustard
- 1 tbsp olive oil
- 4 cups broccoli slaw
- ⅓ cup mayonnaise, sugar-free
- 1 tsp celery seeds
- 1 ½ tbsp apple cider vinegar
- Salt and black pepper, to taste

Directions:
1. Whisk together all ingredients except the broccoli slaw. Place broccoli slaw in a large salad bowl. Pour the dressing over. Mix with your hands to combine well.

Nutrition Info:
- Per Servings 2g Carbs, 3g Protein, 10g Fat, 110 Calories

Shrimp With Avocado & Cauliflower Salad

Servings: 6 | Cooking Time: 30 Minutes

Ingredients:
- 1 cauliflower head, florets only
- 1 pound medium shrimp
- ¼ cup + 1 tbsp olive oil
- 1 avocado, chopped
- 3 tbsp chopped dill
- ¼ cup lemon juice
- 2 tbsp lemon zest
- Salt and black pepper to taste

Directions:
1. Heat 1 tbsp olive oil in a skillet and cook the shrimp until opaque, about 8-10 minutes. Place the cauliflower florets in a microwave-safe bowl, and microwave for 5 minutes. Place the shrimp, cauliflower, and avocado in a large bowl.
2. Whisk together the remaining olive oil, lemon zest, juice, dill, and some salt and pepper, in another bowl. Pour the dressing over, toss to combine and serve immediately.

Nutrition Info:
- Per Servings 5g Carbs, 15g Protein, 17g Fat, 214 Calories

Minty Watermelon Cucumber

Servings: 12 | Cooking Time: 0 Minutes

Ingredients:
- 8 cups cubed seedless watermelon
- 2 English cucumbers, halved and sliced
- ¼ cup minced fresh mint
- ¼ cup balsamic vinegar
- ¼ cup olive oil
- Salt and pepper to taste

Directions:
1. Place everything in a bowl and toss to coat everything.
2. Allow chilling before serving.

Nutrition Info:
- Per Servings 4g Carbs, 0.5g Protein, 8.1g Fat, 95 Calories

Sriracha Egg Salad With Mustard Dressing

Servings: 8 | Cooking Time: 15 Minutes

Ingredients:
- 10 eggs
- ¾ cup mayonnaise
- 1 tsp sriracha
- 1 tbsp mustard
- ½ cup scallions
- ½ stalk celery, minced
- ½ tsp fresh lemon juice
- ½ tsp sea salt
- ½ tsp black pepper, to taste
- 1 head romaine lettuce, torn into pieces

Directions:
1. Add the eggs in a pan and cover with enough water and boil. Get them from the heat and allow to set for 10 minutes while covered. Chop the eggs and add to a salad bowl.
2. Stir in the remaining ingredients until everything is well combined. Refrigerate until ready to serve.

Nutrition Info:
- Per Servings 7.7g Carbs, 7.4g Protein, 13g Fat, 174 Calories

Homemade Cold Gazpacho Soup

Servings: 6 | Cooking Time: 15 Minutes

Ingredients:
- 2 small green peppers, roasted
- 2 large red peppers, roasted
- 2 medium avocados, flesh scoped out
- 2 garlic cloves
- 2 spring onions, chopped
- 1 cucumber, chopped
- 1 cup olive oil
- 2 tbsp lemon juice
- 4 tomatoes, chopped
- 7 ounces goat cheese
- 1 small red onion, chopped
- 2 tbsp apple cider vinegar
- Salt to taste

Directions:
1. Place the peppers, tomatoes, avocados, red onion, garlic, lemon juice, olive oil, vinegar, and salt, in a food processor. Pulse until your desired consistency is reached. Taste and adjust the seasoning.
2. Transfer the mixture to a pot. Stir in cucumber and spring onions. Cover and chill in the fridge at least 2 hours. Divide the soup between 6 bowls. Serve very cold, generously topped with goat cheese and an extra drizzle of olive oil.

Nutrition Info:
- Per Servings 6.5g Carbs, 7.5g Protein, 45.8g Fat, 528 Calories

Crispy Bacon Salad With Mozzarella & Tomato

Servings: 2 | Cooking Time: 10 Minutes

Ingredients:
- 1 large tomato, sliced
- 4 basil leaves
- 8 mozzarella cheese slices
- 2 tsp olive oil
- 6 bacon slices, chopped
- 1 tsp balsamic vinegar
- Sea salt, to taste

Directions:

1. Place the bacon in a skillet over medium heat and cook until crispy. Divide the tomato slices between two serving plates. Arrange the mozzarella slices over and top with the basil leaves. Add the crispy bacon on top, drizzle with olive oil and vinegar. Sprinkle with sea salt and serve.

Nutrition Info:
- Per Servings 1.5g Carbs, 21g Protein, 26g Fat, 279 Calories

Celery Salad

Servings: 4 | Cooking Time: 0 Minutes

Ingredients:
- 3 cups celery, thinly sliced
- ½ cup parmigiana cheese, shaved
- 1/3 cup toasted walnuts
- 4 tablespoons extra virgin olive oil
- 1 tablespoon red wine vinegar
- Salt and pepper to taste

Directions:

1. Place the celery, cheese, and walnuts in a bowl.
2. In a smaller bowl, combine the olive oil and vinegar. Season with salt and pepper to taste. Whisk to combine everything.
3. Drizzle over the celery, cheese, and walnuts. Toss to coat.

Nutrition Info:
- Per Servings 3.6g Carbs, 4.3g Protein, 14g Fat, 156 Calories

Chapter 7: Desserts And Drinks Recipes

Berry Tart

Servings: 4 | Cooking Time: 45 Minutes

Ingredients:
- 4 eggs
- 2 tsp coconut oil
- 2 cups berries
- 1 cup coconut milk
- 1 cup almond flour
- ¼ cup sweetener
- ½ tsp vanilla powder
- 1 tbsp powdered sweetener
- A pinch of salt

Directions:
1. Preheat the oven to 350°F. Place all ingredients except coconut oil, berries, and powdered sweetener, in a blender; blend until smooth. Gently fold in the berries. Grease a baking dish with the oil. Pour the mixture into the prepared pan and bake for 35 minutes. Sprinkle with powdered sugar to serve.

Nutrition Info:
- Per Servings 4.9g Carbs, 15g Protein, 26.5g Fat, 305 Calories

Brownie Fudge Keto Style

Servings: 10 | Cooking Time: 6 Hours

Ingredients:
- ¾ cup coconut milk
- 1 teaspoon erythritol
- 2 tablespoons butter, melted
- 4 egg yolks, beaten
- 5 tablespoons cacao powder

Directions:
1. Mix all ingredients in a slow cooker and cook on low settings for 6 hours.
2. Serve and enjoy.

Nutrition Info:
- Per Servings 1.2g Carbs, 1.5g Protein, 8.4g Fat, 86 Calories

Lettuce Green Shake

Servings: 1 | Cooking Time: 0 Minutes

Ingredients:
- ¾ cup whole milk yogurt
- 2 cups 5-lettuce mix salad greens
- 3 tbsp MCT oil
- 1 tbsp chia seeds
- 1 ½ cups water
- 1 packet Stevia, or more to taste

Directions:
1. Add all ingredients in a blender.
2. Blend until smooth and creamy.
3. Serve and enjoy.

Nutrition Info:
- Per Servings 6.1g Carbs, 8.1g Protein, 47g Fat, 483 Calories

Five Greens Smoothie

Servings: 4 | Cooking Time: 5 Minutes

Ingredients:
- 6 kale leaves, chopped
- 3 stalks celery, chopped
- 1 ripe avocado, skinned, pitted, sliced
- 1 cup ice cubes
- 2 cups spinach, chopped
- 1 large cucumber, peeled and chopped
- Chia seeds to garnish

Directions:
1. In a blender, add the kale, celery, avocado, and ice cubes, and blend for 45 seconds. Add the spinach and cucumber, and process for another 45 seconds until smooth.
2. Pour the smoothie into glasses, garnish with chia seeds and serve the drink immediately.

Nutrition Info:
- Per Servings 2.9g Carbs, 3.2g Protein, 7.8g Fat, 124 Calories

Vanilla Jello Keto Way

Servings: 6 | Cooking Time: 6 Minutes

Ingredients:
- 1 cup heavy cream
- 1 teaspoon vanilla extract
- 2 tablespoons gelatin powder, unsweetened
- 3 tablespoons erythritol
- 1 cup boiling water

Directions:
1. Place the boiling water in a small pot and bring to a simmer.
2. Add the gelatin powder and allow to dissolve.
3. Stir in the rest of the ingredients.
4. Pour the mixture into jello molds.
5. Place in the fridge to set for 2 hours.

Nutrition Info:
- Per Servings 5.2g Carbs, 3.3g Protein, 7.9g Fat, 105 Calories

Vanilla Ice Cream

Servings: 4 | Cooking Time: 50 Minutes + Cooling Time

Ingredients:
- ½ cup smooth peanut butter
- ½ cup swerve
- 3 cups half and half
- 1 tsp vanilla extract
- 2 pinches salt

Directions:
1. Beat peanut butter and swerve in a bowl with a hand mixer until smooth. Gradually whisk in half and half until thoroughly combined. Mix in vanilla and salt. Pour mixture into a loaf pan and freeze for 45 minutes until firmed up. Scoop into glasses when ready to eat and serve.

Nutrition Info:
- Per Servings 6g Carbs, 13g Protein, 23g Fat, 290 Calories

Chocolate Bark With Almonds

Servings: 12 | Cooking Time: 1 Hour 15 Minutes

Ingredients:
- ½ cup toasted almonds, chopped
- ½ cup butter
- 10 drops stevia
- ¼ tsp salt
- ½ cup unsweetened coconut flakes
- 4 ounces dark chocolate

Directions:
1. Melt together the butter and chocolate, in the microwave, for 90 seconds. Remove and stir in stevia.
2. Line a cookie sheet with waxed paper and spread the chocolate evenly. Scatter the almonds on top, coconut flakes, and sprinkle with salt. Refrigerate for one hour.

Nutrition Info:
- Per Servings 1.9g Carbs, 1.9g Protein, 15.3g Fat, 161 Calories

No Bake Lemon Cheese-stard

Servings: 8 | Cooking Time: 0 Minutes

Ingredients:
- 1 tsp vanilla flavoring
- 1 tbsp lemon juice
- 2 oz heavy cream
- 8 oz softened cream cheese
- 1 tsp liquid low carb sweetener (Splenda)
- 1 tsp stevia

Directions:
1. Mix all ingredients in a large mixing bowl until the mixture has a pudding consistency.
2. Pour the mixture to small serving cups and refrigerate for a few hours until it sets.
3. Serve chilled.

Nutrition Info:
- Per Servings 1.4g Carbs, 2.2g Protein, 10.7g Fat, 111 Calories

Mixed Berry Nuts Mascarpone Bowl

Servings: 4 | Cooking Time: 8 Minutes

Ingredients:
- 4 cups Greek yogurt
- liquid stevia to taste
- 1 ½ cups mascarpone cheese
- 1 ½ cups blueberries and raspberries
- 1 cup toasted pecans

Directions:

1. Mix the yogurt, stevia, and mascarpone in a bowl until evenly combined. Divide the mixture into 4 bowls, share the berries and pecans on top of the cream. Serve the dessert immediately.

Nutrition Info:
- Per Servings 5g Carbs, 20g Protein, 40g Fat, 480 Calories

Strawberry Yogurt Shake

Servings: 1 | Cooking Time: 0 Minutes

Ingredients:
- ½ cup whole milk yogurt
- 4 strawberries, chopped
- 1 tbsp cocoa powder
- 3 tbsp coconut oil
- 1 tbsp pepitas
- 1 ½ cups water
- 1 packet Stevia, or more to taste

Directions:

1. Add all ingredients in a blender.
2. Blend until smooth and creamy.
3. Serve and enjoy.

Nutrition Info:
- Per Servings 10.5g Carbs, 7.7g Protein, 49.3g Fat, 496 Calories

Brownie Mug Cake

Servings: 1 | Cooking Time: 5 Minutes

Ingredients:
- 1 egg, beaten
- ¼ cup almond flour
- ¼ teaspoon baking powder
- 1 ½ tablespoons cacao powder
- 2 tablespoons stevia powder
- A pinch of salt
- 1 teaspoon cinnamon powder
- ¼ teaspoon vanilla extract (optional)

Directions:

1. Combine all ingredients in a bowl until well-combined.
2. Transfer in a heat-proof mug.
3. Place the mug in a microwave.
4. Cook for 2 minutes. Let it sit for another 2 minutes to continue cooking.
5. Serve and enjoy.

Nutrition Info:
- Per Servings 4.1g Carbs, 9.1g Protein, 11.8g Fat, 159 Calories

Vanilla Flan With Mint

Servings: 4 | Cooking Time: 10 Minutes

Ingredients:
- ⅓ cup erythritol, for caramel
- 2 cups almond milk
- 4 eggs
- 1 tbsp vanilla
- 1 tbsp lemon zest
- ½ cup erythritol, for custard
- 2 cup heavy whipping cream
- Mint leaves, to serve

Directions:
1. Heat the erythritol for the caramel in a deep pan. Add 2-3 tablespoons of water, and bring to a boil. Reduce the heat and cook until the caramel turns golden brown. Divide between 4-6 metal tins. Set aside and let them cool.
2. In a bowl, mix the eggs, remaining erythritol, lemon zest, and vanilla. Add the almond milk and beat again until well combined.
3. Pour the custard into each caramel-lined ramekin and place them into a deep baking tin. Fill over the way with the remaining hot water. Bake at 345 ºF for 45-50 minutes. Using tongs, take out the ramekins and let them cool for at least 4 hours in the fridge. Run a knife slowly around the edges to invert onto a dish. Serve with dollops of whipped cream, scattered with mint leaves.

Nutrition Info:
- Per Servings 1.7g Carbs, 7.6g Protein, 26g Fat, 269 Calories

Lemon Cheesecake Mousse

Servings: 4 | Cooking Time: 5 Minutes +cooling Time

Ingredients:
- 24 oz cream cheese, softened
- 2 cups swerve confectioner's sugar
- 2 lemons, juiced and zested
- Pink salt to taste
- 1 cup whipped cream + extra for garnish

Directions:
1. Whip the cream cheese in a bowl with a hand mixer until light and fluffy. Mix in the sugar, lemon juice, and salt. Fold in the whipped cream to evenly combine.
2. Spoon the mousse into serving cups and refrigerate to thicken for 1 hour. Swirl with extra whipped cream and garnish lightly with lemon zest. Serve immediately.

Nutrition Info:
- Per Servings 3g Carbs, 12g Protein, 18g Fat, 223 Calories

Choco-coco Bars

Servings: 12 | Cooking Time: 10 Minutes

Ingredients:
- 1/3 cup Virgin Coconut Oil, melted
- 2 cups shredded unsweetened coconut
- 2 droppers Liquid Stevia
- 2 droppers of Liquid Stevia
- 3 squares Baker's Unsweetened Chocolate
- 1 tablespoon oil

Directions:
1. Lightly grease an 8x8-inch silicone pan.
2. In a food processor, process shredded unsweetened coconut, coconut oil, and Stevia until it forms a dough. Transfer to prepared pan and press on the bottom to form a dough. Place in the freezer to set.
3. Meanwhile, in a microwave-safe Pyrex cup, place chocolate, coconut oil, and Stevia. Heat for 10-second intervals and mix well. Do not overheat, just until you have mixed the mixture thoroughly. Pour over dough.
4. Return to the freezer until set.
5. Serve and enjoy.

Nutrition Info:
- Per Servings 4.0g Carbs, 2.0g Protein, 22.0g Fat, 222 Calories

Garden Greens & Yogurt Shake

Servings: 1 | Cooking Time: 0 Minutes

Ingredients:
- 1 cup whole milk yogurt
- 1 cup Garden greens
- 3 tbsp MCT oil
- 1 tbsp flaxseed, ground
- 1 cup water
- 1 packet Stevia, or more to taste

Directions:
1. Add all ingredients in a blender.
2. Blend until smooth and creamy.
3. Serve and enjoy.

Nutrition Info:
- Per Servings 7.2g Carbs, 11.7g Protein, 53g Fat, 581 Calories

Vanilla Chocolate Mousse

Servings: 4 | Cooking Time: 30 Minutes

Ingredients:
- 3 eggs
- 1 cup dark chocolate chips
- 1 cup heavy cream
- 1 cup fresh strawberries, sliced
- 1 vanilla extract
- 1 tbsp swerve

Directions:
1. Melt the chocolate in a bowl, in your microwave for a minute on high, and let it cool for 10 minutes.
2. Meanwhile, in a medium-sized mixing bowl, whip the cream until very soft. Add the eggs, vanilla extract, and swerve; whisk to combine. Fold int the cooled chocolate.
3. Divide the mousse between four glasses, top with the strawberry slices and chill in the fridge for at least 30 minutes before serving.

Nutrition Info:
- Per Servings 3.7g Carbs, 7.6g Protein, 25g Fat, 370 Calories

Baby Kale And Yogurt Smoothie

Servings: 1 | Cooking Time: 0 Minutes

Ingredients:
- ½ cup whole milk yogurt
- ½ cup baby kale greens
- 1 packet Stevia, or more to taste
- 3 tbsps MCT oil
- ½ tbsp sunflower seeds
- 1 cup water

Directions:
1. Add all ingredients in a blender.
2. Blend until smooth and creamy.
3. Serve and enjoy.

Nutrition Info:
- Per Servings 2.6g Carbs, 11.0g Protein, 26.2g Fat, 329 Calories

Ice Cream Bars Covered With Chocolate

Servings: 15 | Cooking Time: 4 Hours And 20 Minutes

Ingredients:
- Ice Cream:
- 1 cup heavy whipping cream
- 1 tsp vanilla extract
- ¾ tsp xanthan gum
- ½ cup peanut butter
- 1 cup half and half
- 1 ½ cups almond milk
- ⅓ tsp stevia powder
- 1 tbsp vegetable glycerin
- 3 tbsp xylitol
- Chocolate:
- ¾ cup coconut oil
- ¼ cup cocoa butter pieces, chopped
- 2 ounces unsweetened chocolate
- 3 ½ tsp THM super sweet blend

Directions:

1. Blend all ice cream ingredients until smooth. Place in an ice cream maker and follow the instructions. Spread the ice cream into a lined pan, and freezer for about 4 hours.

2. Combine all chocolate ingredients in a microwave-safe bowl and heat until melted. Allow cooling. Remove the ice cream from the freezer and slice into bars. Dip them into the cooled chocolate mixture and return to the freezer for about 10 minutes before serving.

Nutrition Info:
- Per Servings 5g Carbs, 4g Protein, 32g Fat, 345 Calories

Raspberry Sorbet

Servings: 1 | Cooking Time: 3 Minutes

Ingredients:
- ¼ tsp vanilla extract
- 1 packet gelatine, without sugar
- 1 tbsp heavy whipping cream
- ⅓ cup boiling water
- 2 tbsp mashed raspberries
- 1 ½ cups crushed Ice
- ⅓ cup cold water

Directions:

1. Combine the gelatin and boiling water, until completely dissolved; then transfer to a blender. Add the remaining ingredients. Blend until smooth and freeze for at least 2 hours.

Nutrition Info:
- Per Servings 3.7g Carbs, 4g Protein, 10g Fat, 173 Calories

Green And Fruity Smoothie

Servings: 2 | Cooking Time: 0 Minutes

Ingredients:
- 1 cup spinach, packed
- ½ cup strawberries, chopped
- ½ avocado, peeled, pitted, and frozen
- 1 tbsp almond butter
- ¼ cup packed kale, stem discarded, and leaves chopped
- 1 cup ice-cold water
- 5 tablespoons MCT oil or coconut oil

Directions:
1. Blend all ingredients in a blender until smooth and creamy.
2. Serve and enjoy.

Nutrition Info:
- Per Servings 10g Carbs, 1.6g Protein, 47.3g Fat, 459 Calories

Dark Chocolate Mousse With Stewed Plums

Servings: 6 | Cooking Time: 45 Minutes

Ingredients:
- 12 oz unsweetened chocolate
- 8 eggs, separated into yolks and whites
- 2 tbsp salt
- ¾ cup swerve sugar
- ½ cup olive oil
- 3 tbsp brewed coffee
- Stewed Plums
- 4 plums, pitted and halved
- ½ stick cinnamon
- ½ cup swerve
- ½ cup water
- ½ lemon, juiced

Directions:
1. Put the chocolate in a bowl and melt in the microwave for 1 ½ minutes. In a separate bowl, whisk the yolks with half of the swerve until a pale yellow has formed, then, beat in the salt, olive oil, and coffee. Mix in the melted chocolate until smooth.
2. In a third bowl, whisk the whites with the hand mixer until a soft peak has formed. Sprinkle the remaining swerve sugar over and gently fold in with a spatula. Fetch a tablespoon full of the chocolate mixture and fold in to combine. Pour in the remaining chocolate mixture and whisk to mix.
3. Pour the mousse into 6 ramekins, cover with plastic wrap, and refrigerate overnight. The next morning, pour water, swerve, cinnamon, and lemon juice in a saucepan and bring to a simmer for 3 minutes, occasionally stirring to ensure the swerve has dissolved and a syrup has formed.
4. Add the plums and poach in the sweetened water for 18 minutes until soft. Turn the heat off and discard the cinnamon stick. Spoon a plum each with syrup on the chocolate mousse and serve.

Nutrition Info:
- Per Servings 6.9g Carbs, 9.5g Protein, 23g Fat, 288 Calories

Almond Butter Fat Bombs

Servings: 4 | Cooking Time: 3 Minutes + Cooling Time

Ingredients:
- ½ cup almond butter
- ½ cup coconut oil
- 4 tbsp unsweetened cocoa powder
- ½ cup erythritol

Directions:
1. Melt butter and coconut oil in the microwave for 45 seconds, stirring twice until properly melted and mixed. Mix in cocoa powder and erythritol until completely combined.
2. Pour into muffin moulds and refrigerate for 3 hours to harden.

Nutrition Info:
- Per Servings 2g Carbs, 4g Protein, 18.3g Fat, 193 Calories

Raspberry Creamy Smoothie

Servings: 1 | Cooking Time: 0 Minutes

Ingredients:
- ¼ cup coconut milk
- 1 ½ cups brewed coffee, chilled
- 2 tbsps raspberries
- 2 tbsps avocado meat
- 1 tsp chia seeds
- 2 packets Stevia or more to taste
- 3 tbsps coconut oil

Directions:
1. Add all ingredients in a blender.
2. Blend until smooth and creamy.
3. Serve and enjoy.

Nutrition Info:
- Per Servings 8.2g Carbs, 4.9g Protein, 33.2g Fat, 350 Calories

Blackberry Cheese Vanilla Blocks

Servings: 5 | Cooking Time: 20mins

Ingredients:
- ½ cup blackberries
- 6 eggs
- 4 oz mascarpone cheese
- 1 tsp vanilla extract
- 4 tbsp stevia
- 8 oz melted coconut oil
- ½ tsp baking powder

Directions:
1. Except for blackberries, blend all ingredients in a blender until smooth.
2. Combine blackberries with blended mixture and transfer to a baking dish.
3. Bake blackberries mixture in the oven at 320°F for 20 minutes. Serve.

Nutrition Info:
- Per Servings 15g Carbs, 13g Protein, 4g Fat, 199 Calories

Chocolate Chip Cookies

Servings: 4 | Cooking Time: 20 Minutes

Ingredients:
- 1 cup butter, softened
- 2 cups swerve brown sugar
- 3 eggs
- 2 cups almond flour
- 2 cups unsweetened chocolate chips

Directions:
1. Preheat oven to 350ºF and line a baking sheet with parchment paper.
2. Whisk the butter and sugar with a hand mixer for 3 minutes or until light and fluffy. Add the eggs one at a time, and scrape the sides as you whisk. Mix in the almond flour in low speed until well combined.
3. Fold in the chocolate chips. Scoop 3 tablespoons each on the baking sheet creating spaces between each mound and bake for 15 minutes to swell and harden. Remove, cool and serve.

Nutrition Info:
- Per Servings 8.9g Carbs, 6.3g Protein, 27g Fat, 317 Calories

30 Day Meal Plan

	Breakfast	Lunch	Dinner
Day 1	Zucchini And Cheese Gratin	Turkey Burgers With Fried Brussels Sprouts	Mixed Roast Vegetables
Day 2	Cranberry Sauce Meatballs	Spicy Sea Bass With Hazelnuts	Spinach Turnip Salad With Bacon
Day 3	Spicy Devilled Eggs With Herbs	Chicken Pesto	Cheesy Cheddar Cauliflower
Day 4	Baked Cheese & Spinach Balls	Rosemary-lemon Shrimps	Turkey Breast Salad
Day 5	Zucchini Gratin With Feta Cheese	Spinach Artichoke Heart Chicken	Roasted Leeks And Asparagus
Day 6	Party Bacon And Pistachio Balls	Pistachio-crusted Salmon	Stewed Chicken Salsa
Day 7	Spinach And Ricotta Gnocchi	Rosemary Grilled Chicken	Sautéed Celeriac With Tomato Sauce
Day 8	Simple Tender Crisp Cauli-bites	Sour Cream Salmon With Parmesan	Cauliflower Risotto With Mushrooms
Day 9	Boiled Stuffed Eggs	Garlic & Ginger Chicken With Peanut Sauce	Paprika 'n Cajun Seasoned Onion Rings
Day 10	Basil Keto Crackers	Tilapia With Olives & Tomato Sauce	Fried Tofu With Mushrooms
Day 11	Garlicky Cheddar Biscuits	Lemon & Rosemary Chicken In A Skillet	Keto Cauliflower Hash Browns
Day 12	Dill Pickles With Tuna-mayo Topping	Shrimp In Curry Sauce	Curried Tofu
Day 13	Spinach Chicken Cheesy Bake	Parmesan Wings With Yogurt Sauce	Cauliflower Fritters
Day 14	Creamy Stuffed Chicken With Parma Ham	Asian Seafood Stir-fry	Crispy-topped Baked Vegetables
Day 15	Avocado And Tomato Burritos	Slow Cooked Chicken Drumstick	Easy Cauliflower Soup

	Breakfast	Lunch	Dinner
Day 16	Berry Tart	Buttery Almond Lemon Tilapia	Stuffed Chicken Breasts With Cucumber Noodle Salad
Day 17	Lettuce Green Shake	Zesty Grilled Chicken	Greek-style Zucchini Pasta
Day 18	Five Greens Smoothie	Thyme-sesame Crusted Halibut	Heart Healthy Chicken Salad
Day 19	Mixed Berry Nuts Mascarpone Bowl	Chicken With Anchovy Tapenade	Greek Salad With Poppy Seed Dressing
Day 20	Zucchini Garlic Fries	Blue Cheese Shrimps	Cauliflower Gouda Casserole
Day 21	Stuffed Portobello Mushrooms	Chicken Cacciatore	Cream Of Thyme Tomato Soup
Day 22	Vegan Cheesy Chips With Tomatoes	Cilantro Shrimp	Warm Baby Artichoke Salad
Day 23	Avocado Salad With Shrimp	Roast Chicken With Herb Stuffing	Simplified French Onion Soup
Day 24	Sushi Shrimp Rolls	Asian-style Steamed Mussels	Caesar Salad With Chicken And Parmesan
Day 25	Tuna Steaks With Shirataki Noodles	Chicken And Mushrooms	Power Green Soup
Day 26	Chipotle Salmon Asparagus	Bacon Wrapped Salmon	Garlic Chicken Salad
Day 27	Red Cabbage Tilapia Taco Bowl	Chicken In Creamy Spinach Sauce	Creamy Cauliflower Soup With Chorizo Sausage
Day 28	Chicken And Bacon Rolls	Chili-lime Shrimps	Pork Burger Salad With Yellow Cheddar
Day 29	Smoked Mackerel Patties	Pancetta & Chicken Casserole	Green Salad With Bacon And Blue Cheese
Day 30	Rosemary Turkey Pie	Salmon And Cauliflower Rice Pilaf	Creamy Cauliflower Soup With Bacon Chips

Chicken And Bacon Rolls 34
Garlic Chicken Salad 62
Chicken Taco Soup 66

Chicken Drumstick

Slow Cooked Chicken Drumstick 27
Chicken Cacciatore 30

Chicken Thighs

Garlic & Ginger Chicken With Peanut Sauce 26
Lemon & Rosemary Chicken In A Skillet 26
Zesty Grilled Chicken 28
Chicken In Creamy Spinach Sauce 31
One Pot Chicken With Mushrooms 32
Caesar Salad With Chicken And Parmesan 62

Chicken Wing

Old Bay Chicken Wings 14
Parmesan Wings With Yogurt Sauce 27

Chocolate

Chocolate Bark With Almonds 75
Choco-coco Bars 78
Vanilla Chocolate Mousse 79
Ice Cream Bars Covered With Chocolate 80
Dark Chocolate Mousse With Stewed Plums 81
Chocolate Chip Cookies 83

Coconut Milk

Brownie Fudge Keto Style 73
Raspberry Creamy Smoothie 82

Cremini Mushroom

Roasted String Beans, Mushrooms & Tomato Plate 19

Cucumber

Greek Salad With Poppy Seed Dressing 58
Minty Watermelon Cucumber 69

D

Dill Pickle

Tuna Topped Pickles 12
Dill Pickles With Tuna-mayo Topping 20

Egg

Spicy Devilled Eggs With Herbs 12
Boiled Stuffed Eggs 18
Sriracha Egg Salad With Mustard Dressing 70

Firm Tofu

Fried Tofu With Mushrooms 54
Curried Tofu 56

Fillet

Spicy Sea Bass With Hazelnuts 45

Goat Cheese

Homemade Cold Gazpacho Soup 70

Greek Yogurt

Mixed Berry Nuts Mascarpone Bowl 76

Ground Turkey

Turkey Burgers With Fried Brussels Sprouts 22

Halibut

Thyme-sesame Crusted Halibut 41

Heavy Cream

Vanilla Jello Keto Way 74

Jumbo Shrimp

Blue Cheese Shrimps 40

Kale

Baby Kale And Yogurt Smoothie 79

Lettuce

Caesar Salad With Smoked Salmon And Poached Eggs 68
Lettuce Green Shake 74

Mackerel

Smoked Mackerel Patties 36

Mascarpone Cheese

Blackberry Cheese Vanilla Blocks 83

Mozzarella Cheese

Strawberry, Mozzarella Salad 65

Mushroom

Turkey & Mushroom Bake 34
Cauliflower Risotto With Mushrooms 50
Stuffed Portobello Mushrooms 50

Mussel

Asian-style Steamed Mussels 39

Pecan

Cajun Spiced Pecans 17

Pork

Pork Burger Salad With Yellow Cheddar 63
Pumpkin & Meat Peanut Stew 66

Raspberry

Raspberry Sorbet 80

Red Cabbage

Red Cabbage Tilapia Taco Bowl 36

Salad Green

Green Salad With Bacon And Blue Cheese 64

Salmon

Chipotle Salmon Asparagus 37
Bacon Wrapped Salmon 39
Sour Cream Salmon With Parmesan 43
Pistachio-crusted Salmon 44
Salmon Panzanella 46

Sausage

Cocktail Kielbasa With Mustard Sauce 18

Scallop

Asian Seafood Stir-fry 42

Shrimp

Chili-lime Shrimps 38
Sushi Shrimp Rolls 39
Avocado Salad With Shrimp 40
Cilantro Shrimp 40
Grilled Shrimp With Chimichurri Sauce 41
Shrimp In Curry Sauce 42
Rosemary-lemon Shrimps 44
Shrimp Spread 45
Brazilian Moqueca (shrimp Stew) 67
Shrimp With Avocado & Cauliflower Salad 69

Spinach

Baked Cheese & Spinach Balls 13
Spinach And Ricotta Gnocchi 15
Greek-style Zucchini Pasta 58
Five Greens Smoothie 74
Green And Fruity Smoothie 81

Strawberry

Strawberry Yogurt Shake 76

Printed in Great Britain
by Amazon

25500000R00053